CAREERCATION

*Trading **Briefcase** for Suitcase*

to Find Entrepreneurial Happiness

DAVID NIU

Founder of TINYhr

CAREERCATION

"Success is not counted by how high you have climbed but by how many people you brought with you."

–Dr. Wil Rose

CAREERCATION

Table of Contents

PREFACE

I've been a serial entrepreneur most of my adult life. My parents emigrated from Taiwan to the U.S. when I was two years old. Since my father was a petroleum engineer, I grew up in Texas and Oklahoma. This means I'm a suffering Dallas Cowboys fan now living in a Super Bowl-proud Seattle Seahawks town.

Along the way, my career would make any "Tiger Mom" proud. After my senior year in Tulsa, I went to U.C. Berkeley for my undergraduate studies. Yes, I did see the "Naked Guy" lollygag around campus during my time there. What an eye-opening experience for a teenager coming from the buckle of the Bible Belt.

I graduated with distinction and joined the prestigious Strategic Services group of Andersen Consulting for three years. I then went to Wharton for my MBA and with a classmate, Andy Liu, I started NetConversions during my first year. We won a Wharton business plan competition and subsequently raised over $1 million from angel investors and venture capital firms like Guy Kawasaki's Garage Technology Ventures. We made our share of mistakes, and the company had a near-death experience, coming close to folding. We came out of that scrape okay, and sold NetConversions to aQuantive (AQNT) in 2004.

After serving as executives at aQuantive, Andy and I took a trip together to Peru. It was either the high altitude, voluminous amounts of beers or the guinea pigs we ate that led us to dream up the next company we'd start together. One caveat we agreed upon: we'd never raise money again. So of course, we turned around and raised over $10 million from tier one investors like Madrona Venture Partners and Charles River Ventures to start BuddyTV in 2005.

Even though it was my own baby, I began to feel burnt out at BuddyTV. I couldn't understand why. BuddyTV operated in a fun and dynamic space combining entertainment with social media. It had a co-founder, board, and team I liked and respected. This conflict completely threw me for a loop: how can someone get burnt out working at his own business?

At the same time, I was also undergoing massive changes in my personal life. I got married and we had our first baby in quick succession. I felt overwhelmed. I decided to break away from my hectic day-to-day schedule and do deep soul searching.

I ended up buying one-way tickets to New Zealand for my wife, baby daughter, and me to travel around the world. I needed to recharge and discover how I could find happiness in my professional and personal life. I called this a careercation (career + vacation). I didn't want to wait until I was in my 60s to travel, when I'd be collecting Social Security and might be in declining health. I'd rather take elongated career breaks throughout my life to gain perspective, connect with my family, and reinvigorate myself.

During the careercation, our young family had two goals while hopscotching around the world. The first was to create some amazing shared family memories with my wife and ten-month-old daughter. The second was more personal: to interview entrepreneurs about leadership, culture, and managing people. As an entrepreneur, my highest highs and lowest lows originate in those areas. I also decided to interview CEOs who were not in the technology space. I wanted to push myself out of my comfortable Seattle technology ecosystem. With the lessons I would learn, I could diversify and grow.

I wrote this book to share my journey towards entrepreneurial happiness via a careercation. I'm also including over two hundred tips that successful entrepreneurs shared with me. These nuggets of wisdom are good for infusing any company with new energy and ideas, and I use quite a few at my new company.

I hope this inspires others to pursue their own path to happiness.

HOW TO READ THIS BOOK

This book is divided into the geographic regions that I visited on my careercation. Each section has an introduction, interviews that I conducted with local entrepreneurs, and my reflections. I recommend reading this book in order; you'll get a pulse on my beliefs throughout the trip. You can also see how the embers of my current endeavor lit up, and how my thoughts on people and culture evolved.

If you want to read a travelogue, you can just stick to the beginning and end of each section. Or if you want to hone in on best practices for managing people, culture, and leadership, then you can just read the interviews. But in keeping with the spirit of my trip, feel free to roam, and don't let the structure hinder you from jumping into any part of the book.

Please note that I conducted these interviews in 2012, so when I say "today," I mean 2012. Some of these companies have grown in size, at least one of them has had to shut their doors, and one of them has been acquired. I also invite you to learn more about each company by checking out their website and following them on Twitter.

Finally, I hope the tips that the business leaders shared inspire you as much as they did me. I left a page for notes after each regional section so you can jot down ideas. Go for it: try some of the suggestions in your own professional and personal journey to find happiness.

THE BEGINNING

"Are you crazy!?"

I was getting used to hearing that when I told my friends and family what I was about to embark on. I sold everything and bought one-way tickets to New Zealand for my wife, our ten-month-old daughter, and me. Not for vacation. Not to live, either. To work? Not exactly.

I decided to take a careercation (career + vacation) and travel around the world with my young family for about six months. After being a hard-charging entrepreneur for over a decade, I was burnt out.

In the past, I'd usually fly somewhere sunny with water, get a bad sunburn, and proclaim myself recharged. I could fool most people with that—but not myself and not this time. I realized that I really needed to slow down before speeding up again.

All About the People

At work, everything looked great. My second startup, BuddyTV, zoomed along full speed ahead. I continued learning new skills like search engine optimization, gamification, and content marketing. Andy Liu—my business partner for my first and second startups—and I celebrated a decade of working together. At this stage in our professional relationship, we could read each other's minds, and we maintained a deep level of trust.

We assembled a great team of folks. This was crucial. Nothing feels better to me than mentoring and coaching employees to harness their untapped potential and exceed all expectations.

At the same time, I'd always assumed that as long as the business was performing well, everyone would be happy, including me. In an attempt to corroborate that, Andy and I conducted our first annual employee survey. I learned to do this from my days as a consultant at Andersen Consulting. We thought if it was good enough for a Fortune 500 company, then it must be good enough for a small startup. In December, we locked ourselves in a room, brought in pizza and cheap beer, and didn't emerge until we concocted fifty questions for a "good" employee survey.

We implored the team to respond by the end of the year. We PowerPointed, pivot tabled, and presented the results in Q1. Then, like most managers do with almost every annual survey, we forgot about the learnings by tax day. Of course, a large annual survey didn't make too much sense since the business—and people's morale—change constantly throughout the year. But we thought we should pattern our practices after Fortune 500 companies.

Then one day, one of the team members pulled me aside to give me two weeks' notice. I felt like I had been stabbed. The news blindsided me. Everyone had seemed happy when we conducted our annual survey. My first thoughts were, *Why are you leaving? Can I save you? Do I want to save you? Is it something I did? Or is it something that I didn't do?*

I offered to change the role and accountabilities for this person. I discussed compensation. I tried everything, but this key member of my team left anyway, which crushed me. In fact, I not only had a mental response but also a physical response. I couldn't sleep well, I had anxiety over who was going to pick up the slack, I was drinking too much, and I was eating poorly. I coined the phrase "34 by 34!" The whole ordeal caused me to drop into such an unhealthy spiral that I started packing on pounds and was forced to buy larger pants. After going from a 30-inch waist to size 32 in short order, I had to draw the line and rally around banning 34-inch waist pants until I was 34 years old.

This wake-up call inspired me to work out and get healthier again. I ran my first half marathon with a dear friend and fellow entrepreneur, Ben Elowitz. I also started meditating and journaling.

During these introspective moments, an important theme came to me. Managing people has been the brightest highlight and also the most maddening frustration of my experience as a serial entrepreneur. The greatest joys in my career have been watching people succeed beyond expectations. The greatest downer is having them fall short of their potential— or leave with no warning. If real estate is all about "location, location, location," then business is all about "people, people, people."

Feeling the Love

In 2009, after completing the Portland Marathon, I celebrated by flying to Saigon to visit my friend Dave Hajdu. Dave had moved to Vietnam to start an onshore-offshore software development company called Vinasource.

Near the end of that fun trip, my friend Simon Han contacted me on Facebook to ask if I was single. He wanted to introduce me to someone. I confirmed my single status and asked him to share more about her, since we all know about blind date nightmares. Simon responded that my potential date was an entrepreneur, also went to Berkeley, and was crowned Miss Chinatown USA. I burned into the keyboard, "YES! Please introduce me!"

That's how I met my lovely wife Alice. Alice was Simon's wife's cousin. So now Simon is my cousin-in-law plus a celebrated family matchmaker.

It was love at first sight. My friends used to tell me, "You'll know when you know." I thought that was BS until I saw Alice. We got married in 2010 and had Keira, our daughter, in 2011. These dramatic life changes also drove me to be more intentional about filling my personal and professional life with happiness.

Feeling the Burnout

As all these changes were happening, I realized my energy was extremely low when getting ready to go to work at BuddyTV in the morning. I asked myself, *Are these isolated instances of just being tired?* I realized that wasn't the case.

The trend pointed towards exhaustion after over ten years of sprinting with a pedal-to-the metal mentality as an entrepreneur. I had to be honest with myself.

I confided to Andy about these feelings and my need to walk away from BuddyTV to recharge. If I couldn't radiate positive energy at work, how could I expect others to do the same? I give Andy tremendous credit for being supportive and understanding about what I needed. We put together a succession plan and pulled off a smooth transition that enabled me to leave BuddyTV in 2012 for my careercation.

Before I left the business, one question kept me awake at night: how could I get so burnt out from a company that I started?

Living Intentionally

- I wish I had let myself be happier.
- I wish I had stayed in touch with my friends.
- I wish I'd had the courage to express my feelings.
- I wish I didn't work so hard.
- I wish I'd had the courage to live a life true to myself, not the life others expected of me.

How many of the above themes can you relate to? If you're like most people, there should be at least a couple of them because these are the top five regrets that people have on their deathbed as documented by Bronnie Ware, a palliative care nurse. Imagining myself near death and thinking through my regrets triggers me to live intentionally.

Alice and I took a course by Seattle relationship guru, John Gottman, who famously determined that there are seven important steps for a successful marriage. The most aspirational one is learning and making your partner's dreams come true.

On that note, when Alice was still in nesting mode around the birth of our daughter, I sheepishly brought up the fact that a dream of mine was to go on a careercation. I shared that some of my best and most formative experiences in life were backpack traveling and studying abroad. In particular, I remembered my junior year studying at Peking University. I didn't have a lot of money, but meeting new people from around the world and experiencing the culture on a native level made me so happy.

Alice quizzed me by noting that buying one-way tickets for a free flowing careercation was a non-intuitive approach for a maniacal planner like me. I agreed. I explained that it was exactly why I needed to do this—to break out of my comfortable Seattle structure and bubble.

She loved me and wanted to support my dreams. She wanted to model living courageously to our daughter Keira. If we're not somewhat anxious, then we're not pushing ourselves hard enough to learn and grow.

Careercation Goals

I was ecstatic that Alice was onboard. I give her tremendous credit for supporting me and enabling this extended break. Of course there were many heart-to-heart discussions about budgeting, safety, sanity and how Keira would fare before Alice fully bought in. She knew the trip would help me to break out of my analytical, over-planning style. Yet, I still felt compelled to shoot for two goals during our careercation.

First, I wanted to create amazing shared memories with my young family. In collaboration, Alice and I planned the places we wanted to go personally and as a family. For example, I wanted to go to the Marlborough Valley in New Zealand because I adore their Sauvignon Blancs. Alice wanted to stop by Shenzhen to visit her father and inhale yummy Cantonese food.

Second, I wanted to interview entrepreneurs and leaders about their best practices in leadership, culture, and managing people. My comfort zone in Seattle is technology-related businesses, so I vowed to talk to CEOs who ran other types of companies. The interviews would run the gamut from a winemaker in New Zealand, to the financial services consultant in Korea, to a fruit trader in China.

I was still haunted by losing a key employee out of the blue and how I became burnt out at my own business. I wanted to see if the joys and heartaches felt by these business leaders were also related to the people and company culture. I hoped this opportunity would shed light on my own challenges and somehow inspire my next journey.

The Devil is in the Details

It's one thing to be a single twenty-year-old guy with a suitcase hopscotching around China without a care in the world. It's another to go on a long, complex journey with a baby.

Was this trip ambitious to carry out with a ten-month-old little one? Sure. Some spouses would not be on board with this plan at all, given the many variables and unknowns. Even though Alice was in, she insisted on one condition: we needed a travel au pair as another set of hands on our careercation.

This stopped me in my tracks. My romantic ideal of traveling together with our baby—bonding and sharing moments—did not include a stranger living with us day in and out. Bringing along a nanny was not traveling light. It was also another incremental cost as we tried to live frugally. I didn't like the idea at all.

Alice told me to take a deep breath. She reminded me that we would want to do some things just as a couple and have our own adventures. Could we find trustworthy babysitters overseas? That type of bond takes time. Taking care of a baby is a lot of work, and it's constant. Keira was starting to take her first steps. Would this trip be about Alice chasing her around but just in a different part of the world?

She made a strong argument. I wanted us both to have fun and relax, not take our daily routine on the road. I agreed it was a reasonable requirement that made sense, and it turned out to be a great decision. *(Yes honey, I admit it. You were right!)*

Laying the Foundation

Alice put a lot of time and research into finding a great fit for our family through an au pair website. She filtered five hundred applications and screened fifty before finally landing on one that seemed perfect.

My job was to find accommodations. To save money and experience the culture at a local level, we would stay in vacation rentals and rental houses, eschewing hotels. We planned to dive into the culture in an authentic way, living amongst locals, shopping at farmers' markets, and buying coffee at local cafes. Buying our own groceries and cooking our own meals would also be a huge money saver. We also saved money by planning strategic visits to family and friends where we stayed for free.

With proper planning, budgeting, and cost control, anyone can embark on a careercation. Admittedly, we went to expensive countries like New Zealand and Australia, but we could have pared expenses if we'd gone to regions like South America or Southeast Asia. I'm convinced that if you put your mind to something, you can achieve it. There are options for traveling on any budget or lifestyle.

We vowed to pack lightly, even though babies need their own battery of gear. I'm proud to say we achieved our goal with only two large suitcases, filled to—but not exceeding—the fifty-pound airline limit. And a medium suitcase. Plus a stroller, car seat, diaper bag, and Pack n Play.

Feeling the Anxiety

Wayne Gretzky said, "You miss 100% of the shots you don't take."

There's always an excuse not to exercise, eat healthy, tackle a bucket list item, or in our case, travel. It's always about leaving your comfort zone. We were determined to follow through.

To ensure that the start date of our careercation wouldn't slip away, I anchored the beginning of our trip to an Entrepreneurs' Organization (EO) conference in Queenstown, New Zealand. Buying the tickets to this event made our commitment concrete and real. Without that commitment, I'm sure we would have been tempted to push back for a variety of reasons.

Truth be told, I felt more nerves, anxiety, and butterflies this time than I ever had for any other trip, including my wedding! But after selling most of our things and storing only a few essential belongings, the liberation from "stuff" combined with our pending trip turned the nerves into excitement.

When the door to the Air New Zealand plane sealed shut, I finally exhaled. Along with the feeling of wheels speeding on the runway came youthful energy that cascaded over me. After living with so much structure and routine in our careers and in parenthood, a careercation would break us out of our comfort zone and push us into the flow to grow. We didn't want to look back on our lives with longing and regret. We were going to take the shot, even while everyone was thinking we were crazy.

①

New Zealand

As I mentioned, lots of people dream of taking an extended trip or moving overseas but often find a reason not to go. One life event or another sways folks into maintaining the status quo. That's why it was important for me to charge my credit card for a conference in Queenstown, New Zealand. This locked in my commitment.

I've been a member of Entrepreneurs' Organization (EO) for a decade. It's a valuable group of entrepreneurs who support each other in their personal and professional growth. EO holds international learning events called Universities, and in 2012, it just happened to be in Queenstown, New Zealand in February.

We decided to jump into our travels by escaping the dreary Seattle winter and enjoy the Southern Hemisphere's summer. Before arriving, I reached out to a diverse set of local entrepreneurs explaining my trip and that I wanted to interview them. Most agreed and seemed excited to play a part in our careercation (many longed to do their own too).

I stuck with my goal to interview people outside of my peers in the tech industry. I talked to a spectrum of Kiwi business leaders: a food-catering TV celebrity, husband-wife recruiters, an artsy new-media design agency diva, a bartending school impresario, a mobile-tech startup inventor, and a yogi vintner.

Between interviews, we experienced New Zealand's natural beauty and visited fun tourist activities like sheep farms and geothermal glaciers. Starting in an English-speaking country eased us into the trip, but island living occasionally shocked my system. Learning that a small can of Coke costs $4 meant kicking my soda habit and switching to coffee to save money.

But the most challenging habit to break was constantly being "on" with emails, texts, Internet, and calls. Alice and I bought SIM cards for our phone only for emergencies. So we gave up Internet and telecommunication access cold turkey.

It was particularly hard, as an entrepreneur for the past dozen years, to unplug. I felt part of my identity and feeling of self-worth was tied to being constantly in demand. Only after a week or so were the silence and independence freeing. It was good that I went through Internet withdrawal cold turkey because we had no choice but to unplug in the South Island's remote areas.

Travel Au Pair Jackpot

On the family front, a huge highlight included meeting our new travel au pair. Hiring sight-unseen a full-time live-in staff/family member/baby-care-taker is mildly stressful. Back in the U.S., after many emails and Skype conversations, Alice had hired Kayla, a young woman from New Zealand. We immediately hit it off with Kayla when we met in person, and she bonded to Keira with natural ease.

Kayla had experience as a nanny with a local family, but our au pair role particularly excited her. She had recently gone to Thailand (and learned to cook a mean mango chicken dish), and the travel bug bit her. New Zealand is beautiful, but it's an island. Like many young Kiwis, Kayla wanted to travel and explore outside of her country.

Usually au pairs get placed with a family in Seattle or Dallas, or a small town far from any city. Traveling around the world definitely sounded more fun and romantic than those choices. Kayla jumped at our opportunity to work as a travel au pair on a careercation.

For us, having a travel au pair gave our family an important extra set of hands. When necessary, I could focus on my interviews without burdening Alice with all the child-rearing duties. This way, each of us had a chance to appreciate our travels in a meaningful way. Plus we had the freedom to go on some very memorable date nights as we traveled.

All in all, we had a great start to our careercation. Keira was fine-tuning her walking skills at the local park and reveled in all the greenery New Zealand offered. Being in an English-speaking country made the transition pretty smooth for Alice and myself. We immediately liked New Zealand.

Then, I jumped into interviewing some interesting entrepreneurs and soaked in their stories.

THE GREAT CATERING COMPANY:
Bigger and Better

Sue Fleischl

The Great Catering Company

Providing food, beverage, and staff for special events, 18 employees, founded in 1995

Susan "Sue" Fleischl, founder of The Great Catering Company, never thought that she would start her own business. Sue considered herself more of a follower than a leader. This I found hard to believe, since she was so engaging during our interview and her personality filled the room.

Early in her professional life, working at catering companies for other people both abroad and in New Zealand, Sue would always note at the end of the day what went well and how things could be improved. In 1995, Sue decided that she could do things better than the others. She started by buying a stainless steel counter, and she stuck it in her living room. She exhorted herself to think B-I-G and to grow into it. That's how she landed on the name The Great Catering Company, even though it was just Sue and a bench in a small house.

Within a month, Sue landed her first three clients: PWC, Carter Holt Harvey, and Chapman Tripp. She was on her way to greatness.

Today, The Great Catering Company employs eighteen full-time employees and fifty casual staff. Their motto is "serving amazing anywhere." They supply the food, beverage, and staff for corporate events, private parties, and weddings. The emphasis is always on amazing, delicious, high-quality food.

Clients want to work with Sue Fleischl—her name is a brand on its own. She gained some celebrity as a mystery critic on a TV show in New Zealand called *The Kitchen Job*. But the food holds up on its own merit: it's all made onsite at the Great Catering Company kitchen using the freshest possible ingredients.

Everything that Sue does at The Great Catering Company she learned for herself. Since cooking is her passion, the challenging part of running her own business has been what most entrepreneurs confess to struggling with: human resources. As Sue describes the dilemma, "Unless you are trained in HR, how do you really know about it?" Reviews are something that don't just give her a headache figuratively: they actually make her stomach turn with anxiety!

The following are important lessons she has learned in developing reviews, hiring and managing the people that Sue credits as helping make the company "Great."

Owning Employee Reviews

Before running the show by herself, Sue was never subjected to a performance review. So for the first few years at Great Catering, she outsourced the process and then took a course to improve how she conducted reviews. But she continued to find the practice wanting: questions were superficial, and she didn't get enough information from the same questions year after year. Now, she does all of the annual reviews herself for eighteen employees, which is quite a task. Most leaders will only review their own direct reports or a handful of managers at most. But these days, Sue gets much more out of the process, including ample feedback.

Right-Sized Review Investment

Each person gets a week to complete the review form. On average, it takes about two hours to complete. She leverages the form to conduct and dig into the review. Since Sue is selective about how much time she spends with each team member, one review could take one or two hours while a more senior person might require two or three hours. Understandably, she has the emotional stamina to do only one or two a day. On the other hand, a delivery driver might require just a casual conversation. So she tailors the review to the individual's needs.

On occasion, as a curveball, her staff will get a form with their job description and expectations listed along one side.

Sue gives each person about fifteen minutes to rate themselves on a scale of 1 to 10, based on how well they performed the expected duties. If they can't complete this form, Sue sits down and peels back the layers to discover underlying issues.

Separate Performance and Compensation Reviews

Sue doesn't think that performance and compensation reviews should be linked. When people are performing at a high level, she will proactively provide them a raise or bonus. She likes the surprise aspect. Sue definitely dislikes and dispels the notion that a performance review equates to a raise. If somebody expects a pay raise for time put in as opposed to what contribution they made to the company—surprise! Better luck next year.

Bottoms-Up Approach

Sue strategically reviews the more junior folks in the company first before moving up the ladder to review their managers. She receives an amazing amount of insight regarding how the managers are performing, which adds to the data she can leverage when reviewing the managers.

A New Year, a New Surprise

As I mentioned, Sue likes surprises. To this end, she changes her performance review annually to keep people on their toes. This switch yields different insights from the previous years. For example, one year the review focused on providing Sue feedback on her personal performance. This included commentary on how well Sue was communicating the vision, goals, and expectations of the company. Another year, the review focused more on peer assessments.

Open Family Atmosphere

The Great Catering Company schedules offsite events for team-building at least twice a year. They've done events like horseback riding and paintball (Sue was a popular target for the paint). Sue is happy to pitch in with chores like mopping and sweeping, and claims that she's still the fastest chopper in the kitchen. Closed doors would create barriers in this environment. Instead, it's a place where everyone sits and works together like a big family. In fact, a lot of the workers call her "Ma."

Personality Tests

When interviewing candidates, The Great Catering Company administers a color profile/personality test from a consulting firm. When Sue took the test, she was designated a very strong red and green, which means that she probably intimidates 90 percent of her staff—and maybe even her customers! She now surrounds herself with softer people to balance out her energy. Everyone in the company knows their teammates' colors, which fosters greater understanding and improves communication.

> *I think personality tests are great icebreakers and effective tools to better understand a person's motivation, communication style and personal preferences. We dabbled in DISC and Myers-Briggs tests in my previous companies, and this is something I'd like to investigate and invest in more in my future ventures.*—David Niu

Conclusion

It's amazing that Sue Fleischl took notes on improving processes at the companies she used to work for, yet never thought about starting her own business. But when she did start The Great Catering Company from her kitchen, she wasn't afraid. She aimed for the stars and already had a lot of ideas about how to do things. Now, she's appeared on TV and is a two-time winner of the Lewisham Caterer of the Year Award. Like most successful entrepreneurs, she thinks fast and constantly tries to make things better. It reminds me of how important it is to think positively and future-proof your company by looking ahead, envisioning where you want to be, and taking the steps necessary to get there.

BKA INTERACTIVE:
One Size Does Not Fit All

Barb Anderson

bka interactive

Full-service digital agency, 14 employees, founded in 2000

Barbara "Barb" Anderson is the bubbly, outgoing type who seems to follow fun—or does fun follow her? She attended University of Otago, New Zealand's party school, infamous for its wild student life. She studied education and went on to teach while starting a family, but the puzzle pieces of her life just didn't fit. Teaching was not for her. Restless from the rigmarole, she quit after her youngest child was born. She returned to school to study art.

Barb had a fantastic time at art school, reveling in contemporary mediums such as digital video and developing an appreciation for technology. Her friend, "a bigwig at Saatchi & Saatchi," persuaded Barb to help on the production side of his firm. Barb, who recognized fun when she saw it, knew that she would have a steep learning curve but likened the challenging ramp-up to puzzle-solving.

Well, she must have been really good at solving puzzles, because shortly after her time at Saatchi & Saatchi, she started bka Interactive.

Founded in 2000 from her kitchen counter, bka now employs fourteen people and is an award-winning full-service digital agency that helps clients in all aspects of growing their business online, from website development to social media to building apps.

Initially, Barb thought she'd be at a huge disadvantage as a woman in her forties in the digital space. But she quickly learned that she was a relatable relief to clients, who dreaded getting design advice from a hipster-clothing-wearing-kid telling them they'd gotten their media strategy all wrong.

Since Barb hadn't spent much time working at big companies, most of the processes that underpin bka's success come from her being nimble, casual, and adaptable.

Here are some insights into how her casual approach has worked.

People, people, people

One of the key strategic moves in bka's success: hire the right people from the get-go. She started the agency by hiring those who could do a better job than she could. Barb speaks affectionately about the quirky personalities on her team; it's clear that she has built the company's processes around them rather than trying to fit people into pre-set routines.

Because of New Zealand's strict labor prohibitions against firing workers without numerous formal warnings, procedures, and mediation meetings, hiring the right person from the start is critically important to all Kiwi companies. However, a recent "three-month trial period" that the country implemented has helped employers like Barb to relax about hiring. While nobody has left bka within that trial period, Barb and other small-business owners don't feel like they are taking an enormous risk when bringing on someone new. Nonetheless, screening for the best fit is built into a culture like bka's.

The Best Laid Schemes of the Digital World

Barb sees no need to hold annual strategic meetings, because in a fast-moving, dynamic industry such as hers, what's hot today could very well be replaced in six months by a more interesting opportunity. Instead, strategic planning happens often, as workload and production dictate. She thrives on this spontaneity. No recurring lesson plans for bka!

Rolling Feedback and Bonuses

Barb is a big believer in providing constant feedback instead of bottling it all up for the annual review. She does this verbally and also through frequent bonuses to employees who exceed expectations. With a profitable company and low turnover, Barb wants to share the success with those responsible.

"Outsourcing" Performance Reviews

Barb has created a laid-back work environment and enjoys her friendly, casual bka relationships. Everyone sits together in an open-bullpen arrangement, so she hates the idea of sitting across from someone to critique their work formally in a review setting. However, she has recognized the value that such an arrangement holds for her staff: quality one-to-one communication on issues that perhaps have gone unaddressed. So Barb decided to delegate all of the performance reviews to her GM.

This way, Barb is not directly involved, and she minimizes the dread or discomfort associated with the process.

Career Ownership

Barb combines the performance review and compensation review and focuses the meeting on understanding where the reviewee wants to go in their career. Barb believes people should leave bka "equipped to enter their dream job." So bka people are encouraged to own their career and find courses to help—the agency pays for training that will get staff members where they want to go.

No One-Size Fits All

Being an agency, bka has its share of unusual, creative personalities. Some of these folks don't want to "play the game" and do a formal review process. They just want another raise. For these employees, Barb amends the process to fit the situation. She truly thinks that the process needs to be flexible.

Giving to Each Other

I got a bit of an education and a huge smile when Barb shared that someone on the team is randomly selected to make tea for their coworkers every Friday. A typical American might wonder, "How do you 'make' tea? Offer selections like green tea, Earl Grey, lemon? How difficult can it be?"

Actually, making tea for the Kiwis at bka is a very involved process. First, the randomly chosen team member has to hand-make the cake, goodies, or sandwiches by themselves. No outside help is allowed. Second, if you do a poor job, you'll definitely hear about it! Friday Tea is a huge hit now, and everyone strives to outdo the others. What a great example of how culture isn't just about the company giving, but also about employees giving to one another—and having a hoot along the way.

> *I love this idea! We hosted potluck holiday parties at BuddyTV, and they were always a hit; people would anonymously submit their dishes to be voted on by their peers. Coworkers were quite competitive whipping out secret family dishes for the win. I must admit that I finished 1st one year and 2nd the following year. Thanks for the winning recipes, Mom.*—David Niu

Conclusion

From an unconventional path to starting bka, Barb has instilled a unique and flexible approach throughout her company. They don't impose a rigid one-size-fits-all review process on everyone. Even more thought-provoking is the notion that bka provides continuous feedback, plus bonuses and raises when merited, throughout the year.

Every company will develop a culture whether its leaders are proactive in shaping it or not. So why not be proactive in guiding it? Most impressive is how the culture is now baked in to bka, and how employees have taken the lead themselves with Friday Teas and Dress-Up Fridays. Those particular events wouldn't work for everybody, but Barb has tailor-made a culture that suits not just her but also the talent she's selected to help her succeed.

THE PROFESSIONAL BAR AND RESTAURANT SCHOOL:

A Fire Starter who Hires Others Well to Tend the Flames

Luella Bartlett

The Professional Bar and Restaurant School

Hospitality training services, including cooking, food and beverage, and hotel management, 54 employees, founded in 1993

Luella Bartlett admits that in her younger days, she was a shockingly poor employee who always thought that she knew best. So it's probably a good thing that she fell into starting her own business, The Professional Bar and Restaurant School (PBRS), with her husband, Scott.

Scott founded the company in 1993 when he bought it for $500 from a friend who wanted to windsurf more. At that time, the company was a one-man-band that taught two-week bartending courses. Luella Bartlett joined PBRS in 1998, and they began to expand aggressively.

Today, PBRS employs fifty-four people in two locations and provides hospitality-training services to international students for the global industry. Their services include courses on cooking, food and beverage, and hotel management. Moreover, they help most students attain a position in the industry for twenty hours per week while they're studying.

It's funny that Luella was once a nightmare employee, because as a business owner, she is really on top of her game. It takes innovation and leadership to turn a tiny how-to business into a full-fledged college that follows government compliance and attracts an international student body.

Keeping The Professional Bar and Restaurant School as a leader in the industry is no small task. Luella shared the following management and leadership best practices.

Accountability for All

The PBRS executive management team regularly meets with a governance board of directors, which includes KPMG. Annually, they conduct a strategy planning session, and PBRS leadership meets with the board once a month to report on progress. In fact, each department head must also provide monthly updates on metrics and Key Performance Indicators (KPIs).

Since entrepreneurs are usually the boss, they often don't answer to anyone. Some like it that way. That's why they start their own businesses. Others crave a mechanism for keeping themselves accountable. One of the reasons why PBRS is so successful is that Luella finds accountability through her governance board to objectively measure, monitor, and improve their business performance.

Know Thyself

Luella Bartlett considers herself a "fire-starter": she thinks of great ideas but knows that only by hiring the right people will her vision come to fruition. Well-aware of her personal weaknesses, Luella has brought a GM onboard to oversee management and implementation of strategy. It's clear that this ability to put her ego aside has helped the company to run more efficiently.

Leverage IT

Recently, PBRS has implemented some great systems and technologies to streamline communication and processes. For HR, Luella leverages Sonar6, an online HR solution that everyone in the company uses to input and receive feedback on their performance.

A performance review usually takes only twenty minutes using this tool because the feedback between staff and manager is accessible online prior to the face-to-face meeting. The bulk of the in-person review then covers discrepancies and formalizes growth and career opportunities in the staffers' personal development plans.

Separate Performance and Compensation Review

In the past, PBRS conducted both of these reviews at the same time, but Luella discovered that people expected a compensation increase whether or not they had done a good job, regardless of the company's financial performance. They now hold pay reviews once a year, in January. Performance reviews may be quarterly, with some biannually, depending on the position. Since separating the two, Luella feels much better. She feels that the company still hasn't hit on the perfect process for evaluating compensation, but they're constantly reviewing and trying to improve.

No Reviews = No Pay Increase

Many companies suffer from overdue performance reviews. To combat this, Luella implemented a policy whereby managers don't receive their own review and pay increases until they've completed their staff reviews. She posts online the completed reviews and those that still need to be done, creating a powerful peer-pressure incentive to complete staff reviews on time. Only after all reviews are done can managers then receive a review of their own performance.

> *I think this is a brilliant idea. I've known organizations that have dragged reviews from Q1 into Q2. But aligning a manager's own review with their team's review is commonsensical and easy.*
> *—David Niu*

Seek Consistency Across Departments

Luella admits that, across all departments, compensation grading needs better consistency. They're able to map the performance of every employee on a grid, and it becomes clear which managers are more generous in their evaluations. They're continually monitoring and improving this process; the HR manager is taking courses and plans to train the managers on how to do it better.

Hire People that Fit the Culture

Since people are among PBRS's most important assets, Luella is committed to hiring based on cultural fit. "Skills can be taught," she reasons. However, people either click with a given culture or they don't.

Conclusion

Luella and her husband have created a winning combination. Recognized as the supreme winner of the Westpac Waitakere Business Awards, PBRS attracts students from all over the world, especially from countries that have developing service economies like China and India. I found it interesting how those qualities which are so important to being the best in the hospitality industry—innovation, leadership, and staff—are what have propelled PBRS to success. The IT tools that Luella uses help ease the HR dilemmas that drive other managers to the brink of madness, and these techniques enable her to focus on the vision of her business's future growth.

WORKING IN:
Paddling their Own Canoe to Success

Scott and Hayley Roberts

Working In

Online jobs marketplace
connecting international
candidates with potential
employers, 37 employees,
founded in 1998

Scott and Hayley Roberts were working at competing marketing companies in London when they met at a business conference in Hong Kong. By the time they started dating, Scott had become increasingly disenchanted with the strangling routine of his day job. One night, while watching a documentary on the wealthiest people in the UK, Scott was jolted with inspiration when one of the billionaires being interviewed advised viewers to "paddle your own canoe if you want to get rich." At that moment, Scott realized that he wasn't going to earn real wealth as an employee. He knew he had to start his own business. Meanwhile, Hayley had hit a wall in her own job. She'd risen up the ranks, yet even with her ideas and energy, she now had nowhere to go within the organization.

Scott wanted to return to New Zealand, and Hayley was keen to try working there. They hit upon the right idea at the right time: a magazine for employers to lure skilled Kiwi labor back home from overseas. The couple took a two-week "vacation" to New Zealand to gauge interest, and employers jumped at the opportunity to advertise. Upon returning to London, they quit their jobs and started Working In in 1998.

Today, Working In employs thirty-seven people in New Zealand and overseas, with additional offices in Sydney, London, Johannesburg, and Brazil. It provides an online marketplace for international candidates to meet potential employers in a destination country, and permits employers to search globally for talent. The company also hosts more than ten employment expos around the world annually.

Most of the employers that use these services are in the engineering, mining, and natural resource industries, with typical salaries starting in the six-figure range.

Scott and Hayley acknowledge having felt growing pains a few years back, when the global recession closed a heavy door on their clients' recruitment costs and international travel budgets. Working In had been growing aggressively, "charging ahead way too fast to stop immediately," Hayley admits. Rather than let this financial hiccup stop their plans, they formalized their strategic planning and brought in outside investment. To align the goals of the company's founders and investors, Scott and Hayley disciplined themselves to create an operational plan, brought in an HR manager when the company hit around twenty-five hires, and scaled back on the number of expos. The company is now back on track to grow at a healthy clip.

Drawing on the wisdom from fourteen successful years, they relayed the following insights for other entrepreneurs to learn from.

Separate Performance and Compensation Reviews

Scott believes that performance reviews shouldn't be clouded by money. Everyone should be able to talk freely and discuss where they want to go in their careers.

Separating a performance review from one for salary upgrades provides an opportunity to hold a frank discussion without the pressure of pay looming over anyone's head. Additionally, it affords the managers time to implement whatever structure is required to elevate that employee to his or her next level in pay.

No More 360s

Working In conducted 360-degree peer reviews in the past. In HR lingo, "360" reviews are a popular employee development tool: peers provide feedback to one another, and to their employers. The staff was at first skeptical and nervous, but then they all submitted glowing feedback about one another that didn't provide much value to the founders—but it did create more paperwork.

Make the Right Hire the First Time

Hayley shared that Working In screens new hires for a positive attitude, because with the right mindset they can easily train people in the needed skills. But the opposite doesn't work for them. For key positions at the company, Scott would forsake growth and profitability to wait until the very best person could fill the role. How many of us have hired someone less than perfect because we desperately needed someone in that seat—and came to regret that hasty decision later?

First Interview = 20 Minutes

Their first in-person interview is only twenty minutes, and like with "speed dating," the founders know very quickly if they click with the person. If there's good chemistry, then the candidate comes back for a longer second interview.

> *For most of my interviews, I start with an online exercise that evaluates if candidates can follow directions and perform under a time constraint. Then my first interview takes usually forty-five to sixty minutes. I think the twenty minute "speed dating" makes a lot of sense either on the phone or in person to quickly ascertain fit.*
> *—David Niu*

Leverage Personality Testing

After the second interview, Working In leverages ASSESS as their personality test for candidates and how they may fit in a particular role. Scott thinks this isn't as easy to interpret as the DISC system of testing people's personalities, but he really likes it for people in sales roles. Hayley agrees that DISC has a wider reach, and is more applicable especially for team dynamics and how to deal with one another.

Conduct Annual Company Survey

Working In participates in an annual survey conducted through the Kenexa Best Workplaces program, which accrues anonymous employee feedback on eighty-six areas of management.

Respondents answer, on a 1-to-5 point scale, such questions as:

- "Do you know your role?"
- "Would you recommend someone else to work at your company?"
- "Do you know the strategy of the company?"

If 80 percent of the company responds, the organization can compete with other local businesses for the designation of "Best Company to Work For." The results come back on a scorecard that highlights areas for concern and improvement along with qualitative feedback in all eighty-six areas. Kenexa's program works so well for Working In that the employees actually ask to participate every year. Scott and Haley are proud to score in the above-average range and are especially thrilled to have this level of engagement from employees. And the feedback is valuable.

A Team is a Team

Because the founders take care to make the right hire from the get-go, they feel comfortable keeping communication frank and open between themselves and with employees. As Scott put it, "In a sports team or with flat-mates, if your teammates don't buy into who you are, it's pretty hard to change. Ask for feedback and encourage it. Getting it up front mitigates most issues."

But like any team, even the founders have contrasting views on communication and reviews. While Scott is okay with the casual huddle approach, Hayley understands that her staff may crave more formal reviews as a pathway to growing; she links this sentiment to happiness and retention.

Conclusion

This was my first interview with a husband-wife team that ran a company together. This couple complemented one another and finished each other's sentences during the interview. As expected for a company in the employment industry, Scott and Hayley provided some great tips for other businesses that seek to grow, especially in the screening and hiring process.

STONYRIDGE VINEYARD:
You Don't Get Reviewed in Nirvana

Steve White

Stonyridge Vineyard

Wine export, agriculture, restaurant, 35 employees, founded 1981

Steve White was busy having adventures after university when he gradually developed a reverence for wine. He studied horticulture, worked in wineries in California and Italy, and skippered yachts. Returning to New Zealand after a big worldwide yacht race, Steve was inspired to bring the culture and lifestyle of the great Mediterranean vineyards to his home country. Steve found his destiny on Waiheke Island, and started Stonyridge Vineyard there in 1981.

Steve describes the business as a full agriculture, restaurant, exportation, and government compliance operation. Stonyridge Vineyard, surrounded by verdant rolling hills and flanked by beautiful white-sand beaches, employs thirty-five people in a very casual, family-like atmosphere.

Stonyridge is not a corporate-style business. Perhaps it is the outdoor setting, or maybe it's the Mediterranean aspect of a winery, or just Steve's laid-back approach to business that makes it that way. Regardless of how the company culture has evolved, Steve has created a successful place to work. Over a delicious lunch, he shared the following insights on people management.

Nobody Wins in Performance Reviews

Nobody really likes performance reviews, but Steve sees absolutely no value in their current state. He feels that any formal review is somewhat confrontational and creates unhealthy expectations for a raise. In his view, reviews are time consuming, take a short-sighted view backwards, and create a lose-lose situation. Either the employee is denied a wage increase, gets frustrated, and negatively affects the company going forward; or the employer feels bad because he has been backed into a corner—possibly at a vulnerable moment in the business—and reluctantly gives a raise just to avoid a mess.

Walk Softly and Carry No Stick

Part of Steve's terrible experience with reviews has to do with labor laws in New Zealand. In the United States, the typical employment agreement is based on at-will employment. Basically, both the employer and employee can leave the agreement with or without cause. Steve likens performance reviews in the U.S. to walking softly yet carrying a big stick. As he puts it, "you can do a job review that on the surface is very nice and politically correct, and end it with 'sorry, empty your desk; you've lost your job.' That's a big stick."

In New Zealand, it's illegal to fire a worker in a similar fashion. For example, people have been caught on camera stealing and have still successfully sued their employers for improper dismissal. The picture he painted for me is, "imagine an underperforming employee. If you give him a harsh review, he'll just be more disgruntled and disruptive, with very little recourse for the employer." This is a major reason performance reviews are much more challenging to conduct in a more regulated workforce setting: in terms of discipline, the assessments don't have any teeth.

Strong Bonus System

Steve has implemented a robust bonus system at Stonyridge Vineyard. He'd prefer to abandon the review system for a transparent bonus system based on what value each person brings into the business. He might opt to give someone a bonus or pay raise spontaneously for a job well done.

Management Minimalism

Steve hires people to lead smaller teams and prefers to be a communication conduit between junior seasonal staff and their managers. The leaders follow the golden rule "praise publicly and admonish privately." It seems to work well, as Steve says there are very few problems with employees. He can gauge their happiness by the energy they bring to their customer interactions.

Teach Your Staff Yoga

Steve is a yoga instructor as well and began providing free yoga classes to his staff three years ago. His eyes lit up during the interview when he began describing the massively positive effects teaching yoga has had on the company.

As a yoga instructor, his approach is about service to his students as individuals. The bond between the yoga teacher and pupil is very caring and creates enormous loyalty. The team loves the yoga classes, and Steve claims that yoga solves all problems.

Rather than subjecting everyone to formal reviews and "PC" processes, Steve describes this scenario: "A staff yogi would work really hard and show loyalty, and if they have that integrity, when they approach you for a pay raise, maybe you recognize that they are right, but you still can't afford the increase. Then they might suggest that they have to leave and make more money elsewhere, but will commit to giving you ample time to find a replacement." No hard feelings, mutual respect, good vibes.

Conclusion

Borrowing a line from the popular Dos Equis beer commercials, Steve White must be "the most interesting man in New Zealand." Instead of a lager, however, he'll hoist a glass of fine Stonyridge Vineyard wine.

To counter the negativity around performance reviews, he's instituted a strong bonus system and teaches his workers yoga.

I was so intrigued after hearing that Steve created more loyalty from his staff by teaching them yoga that I asked, curiously, "so what's next?" hoping to learn and share the next big people management trend. Steve smiled and replied, "Death."

I definitely won't be teaching anyone yoga anytime soon as I struggle to touch my toes. Yet, similar to doing group exercise like yoga, my friend's company trained and completed a Tough Mudder race together. There was an immense amount of preparation, teamwork, and camaraderie. I'll look to sponsoring groups of employees to train for a race or athletic event because I've seen the positive vibes and bridges it builds outside the workplace.
—David Niu

DYNAMITE:
Evolves and Ignites

Mat Wylie

DYNAMITE

Mobile marketing
technology developer, 5
employees, founded 1995

Mat Wylie has only had one job interview in his life, and he got that job when he was nineteen. Just a few years later, a partner at the ad agency that employed him wanted Mat and two others to buy him out for $250,000. Mat jokes that they probably didn't even have $25 amongst them—much less $250K.

Instead, the three of them started Dynamite in 1995. Dynamite has evolved significantly over the past seventeen years. Like a comet approaching the sun, it shed some layers as it got brighter and more focused. First, it started as a full-service advertising agency. Second, after six years, they bought out one partner who moved to Singapore. Third, after eleven years, Mat Wylie bought out the remaining partner,

Fletch, who left to run his family business and pursue his passion for flying. Fourth, Mat transformed Dynamite into a product company from its roots as a service agency.

Dynamite is now in mobile marketing with multiple product offerings using emerging technology. Their core product, Customer Radar, is revolutionizing the mystery-shopper industry. It's a mobile technology that enables retailers to collect live feedback from customers in their store in exchange for a chance to win a prize, like an iPad. Instead of relying on one mystery shopper's opinion, retailers can now collect hundreds and thousands of ratings and high-quality feedback from actual store traffic.

It wasn't always the smoothest process, transitioning from a service-based business to a product-based one. But Mat knew that he had to do it after a long-standing, satisfied customer received orders from global headquarters to change their ad agency because "change is needed for the sake of change; that's just what you do." Mat sensed it would be too hard to grow a business built strictly on ideas.

Mat clearly remembered the epiphany he had years ago at an Entrepreneurs' Organization retreat. He recited from memory the goal he set there: "I want to transform Dynamite from a service-based business to a product-based business that can be used anywhere around the world." He questioned himself many times through this challenging transformation, but he stuck to his vision. Now Dynamite is at a tipping point with Customer Radar gaining significant traction.

Dynamite employs five people, and Mat likes their casual, family-like environment. Having a limited number of employees allows Dynamite to stay nimble. He does admit that the atmosphere will need to change as they grow. In the meantime, Mat shared the following tips and experiences.

Founder Accountability

For many years, Mat had partners, and they were all accountable to one another, but now he is the only one in charge. However, under New Zealand law, Mat's wife—married to the sole shareholder—owns 50 percent of Dynamite. She acts like a business partner and helps keep him on track. At one point, Mat had three great ideas but limited resources. Mrs. Wylie held Mat's feet to the proverbial fire and made him commit to only one—much like their courtship, which also resulted in a successful partnership. Well played, Mrs. Wylie!

Mat also has an invaluable community with his Entrepreneurs' Organization network. He founded an EO Forum with other members. Together they created a superbly well-attended offsite event for global members to network and absorb knowledge from other business leaders. His fellow forum founders have helped him with HR issues, and he feels the accountability and support they provide have helped him tremendously.

Separate Performance and Compensation Reviews

Dynamite conducts compensation reviews once a year on the employee's anniversary date. The performance review happens about three to four months prior to the compensation review because this gives the employee a chance to hit goals and showcase their value to garner a raise.

Mat dislikes the expectation of a raise just because a performance review happens. He likes compensation awards to be based on actual performance. At the same time, his team knows they can make large jumps in salary based on performance rather than just smaller, incremental increases.

Crystallize Your Vision

Mat Wylie was the chair for the extremely successful EO University Queenstown event that brought entrepreneurs from around the world to New Zealand. His vision for the event was to create "Four hundred raving fans of all things Kiwi." Everyone on board bought into this plan, and the vision also rallied support from sponsors like Air New Zealand. The vision was clear, short, simple, and effective.

Mat admits he learned a key lesson for Dynamite when chairing the EO University. He's reevaluating Dynamite's vision to make it razor sharp and clear, like the one he formulated for the forum. It worked for him when he changed the business model of the company from service to product, so now it's time to look ahead.

Relax and Focus on Results

He admits that in the past, he felt irritated when workers came in late or left early. Now he's more laid-back and focuses on results instead. Employees now come in after traffic dies down, which helps morale and increases productivity—a true win-win.

Avoid Ranking Employees

Mat doesn't quantitatively rank his employees' performances, nor does he force them to rate themselves. He doesn't feel that's the Dynamite way. He also concedes that his approach may be culture-specific, because Kiwis are less aggressive and confrontational than other parts of the world are.

Constant Feedback

Since Dynamite is more personal than formal, everyone receives continuous feedback. Mat won't wait until a structured review to deal with someone's performance. Since the company is small, there is always time for a chat.

Discipline the Behavior, not the Person

For anyone who needs to critique another, be it parent-child, teacher-student, or manager-employee, a good adage to remember: "Discipline the behavior, not the person." Mat compartmentalizes the behavior from the person, so his criticism can't be construed as a personal attack.

To illustrate, he may say, "When we take a condescending tone with our suppliers, it doesn't align with Dynamite's core values and isn't productive. Moving forward, I'd like for this behavior to change so everyone whom we work with will have a pleasant experience with our brand." He has had success with this approach. Down the road, his team appreciates the personal growth that such a style encourages.

> *I'm a fan of this approach. I disdain passive-aggressive behavior, so I always seek to engage. This is a good reminder for me to disassociate the behavior from the person since I can get caught up, especially if it's a highly charged issue.*—David Niu

Conclusion

Mat has evolved Dynamite tremendously in the last seventeen years to stay ahead of trends. He's bought out two business partners and moved into an arena (mobile) that wasn't even around when he began the company. Mat freely admits that, as the company grows, they will need to adopt more structure, and he claims that he isn't the one to drive it. One thing that should continue to work well into the future is his open communication style with his team. The constant flow of feedback among everyone in the company, combined with Mat staying true to his vision, has encouraged healthy iterative growth that Dynamite can enjoy for years to come.

NEW ZEALAND IN THE REAR VIEW MIRROR

Starting our adventure in New Zealand, the extreme sport capital of the world, worked well. We got our bearings in Auckland and brought Kayla, our new au pair, on board with us. Ferrying around and exploring the North Island and Rotura by car was a blast. We loved everything from traditional Maori dance performances, glow worm demonstrations at night, Keira laughing and clapping over sheep-shearing, to me burning myself with geothermal sulfur water. It was fun.

Entrepreneurs' Organization flew us on a plane used by the national rugby team the All Blacks to the South Island. Besides business talks, EO organized activities that included adventures like bungee jumping and speed boating. So I kick-started my careercation with great contacts and a shot of adrenaline. Alice and I joked that the Kiwi way is to do something death defying and then say, "Whoa, that was close ... wasn't that awesome!"

Then, back on our own, we switched to a campervan to check out fresh lakes, waterfalls, glaciers, and pristine beaches. This handy vehicle gave us the mobility to check out remote places and spare us hotels. Nevertheless, there were hiccups in figuring out basics, like making the heat operable and learning the value of a flat parking space. Finally, driving a massive campervan around hairpin turns hundreds of feet above the sea made for a literal white-knuckle experience. Going down a one mile, one-way tunnel without the signal lights working on the way to see Milford Sound definitely gave me cold sweats.

Along with adapting to driving this awkward vehicle, Alice and I had to adapt, too, as a couple. We almost killed each other in the campervan's cozy confines. As you can imagine, after having so many outlets for our own separate personal life (sports, jobs, friends), being enclosed in a small box and spending every minute together challenged our usual dynamic.

Not only were Alice and I learning to deal with each other at the start of a supposedly relaxing, fun, and engaging careercation, but we also had to deal with Kayla when she admitted she was homesick and may not be able to continue with us. This caught us flat-footed. We hadn't even left New Zealand yet, and we had thought she was fitting in with us so well.

We thought about it from her point of view. We had been nervous leaving *our* friends, family, and familiar settings behind in Seattle when we jumped. She must've felt the same way. Alice and I talked openly with her, sharing our personal first-time travel experiences—we had been there before and knew what she was feeling. We encouraged her to give it a little bit more time, and we all agreed to have regular check-ins.

Happily for everyone, Kayla trusted us and stayed on for the entire time. A great team player, Kayla also enjoyed some of her own independent travel experiences along the way.

From the beginning, we'd felt that we hit the "nanny jackpot" with Kayla. However, like any successful relationship, it required two-way communication and understanding. I developed a system of check-ins for the three of us. We used this process between Alice and me and among Kayla and us to discuss highs, lows, things that are on the horizon, and topics to discuss. It reminded me of the kind of managing I like to do at work. Only this time, the payoff in creating a positive culture was not financial dividends, but something even greater—happy, relaxed family experiences. It still comes down to people.

Ironically enough, the one adapting the best was little Keira. She celebrated her first birthday at a Christchurch RV park. We had a small pastry while we sang to her—but no candles or gifts. Just plenty of love and one fantastic family moment shared. It taught me without a doubt that having children is no excuse to not travel together: they will be far more adaptable than I am.

Defying the Odds

While driving around the South Island, I had plenty of time to reflect on the interviews I conducted on the North Island. The challenge of running a business from a geographically remote country became apparent to me right away. For example, when I told others how long the flight was from Seattle, I expected some empathy. Instead, Kiwis would deadpan, "Mate, we fly that far every time we go anywhere." I take it for granted that I can hop on a plane and be in New York in about five hours or London and Tokyo in ten hours.

The limited market size in New Zealand also struck me. The Seattle metro area has a population of 3.5 million people. New Zealand as a whole only has 4.4 million. So it's much easier to scale a business in the U.S. when our total domestic market is 314 million people.

Another theme that emerged from my interviews is how laws and regulations impact business practices. The U.S. has relatively lax laws when it comes to employee hiring and firing. Kiwi workers enjoy comparably strong protection. Given the legal obstacles to dismissing an employee in New Zealand, business leaders can't afford to hire someone with the right skills while only hoping that at some point the employee conforms to the company's values. Many entrepreneurs in New Zealand prefer to prioritize a good fit and then train new hires.

The third highlight for me was how quickly these entrepreneurs opened up and shared. I felt like a trusted friend or therapist as they engaged openly. Even though they were all so successful, they never boasted about revenues and profits. Instead, I saw incredible humility. They shared their mistakes and tips, happy to help others who follow in their footsteps.

No Entrepreneur is an Island

I noticed that I wasn't alone in my struggles. My challenge around managing people and the burnout I experienced was not isolated to me. Many had experienced something similar or had transitioned out of it, always striving for more happiness in their personal and work life. They shared the human side of starting and running a business—the hard stuff that's often masked by blogs and books that extol only the fantastic successes. I felt privileged that this group opened up so readily, and I grew even more excited to interview other entrepreneurs in Australia.

Near the closing of the conference, we had the privilege of hearing inspirational international speaker Ngahi Bidois give a gripping motivational talk. Expressing so much wisdom, several times he reiterated the importance of people. He quotes a Maori proverb: "The things I have been pleased and privileged to achieve, are not mine alone, but those of many." It was a fitting theme to embrace at the start of my journey.

②

Australia

We hit Australia in late March. The plan was to immerse ourselves in Sydney for about a month and then head to the Gold Coast and Byron Coast for some fun in the beautiful, beachy sun.

So far, we'd learned some great lessons on the careercation. We didn't need as much stuff as we packed, so we unloaded quite a bit of gear on friends at the EO conference to take back to Seattle for us. The trip gave Alice and me some unexpected spousal challenges we had to work through while campervanning. In hindsight, of course we should've anticipated a little conflict. But sometimes you just don't know what you don't know.

We worked through it, and to this day use the "check in" process that we developed in New Zealand. Kayla gave us another unexpected challenge when she almost left before the trip began. We thereafter remembered to keep a pulse on her needs. In spite of all that, the careercation was overall providing the break I so desperately craved.

With respect to lodging, we had great experiences throughout New Zealand.

However, the worst accommodation and service we experienced on our trip—maybe ever—was at a townhouse we initially rented in Sydney. There were cockroaches scrabbling around, which freaked out Alice. Shards of glass in the carpet freaked me out, since Keira could easily mistake it for food if not step on it. Management was unapologetic and terrible to deal with, which put an initial damper on our spirits.

As they say, "we can't control situations, just how we react to them." We focused on positive thinking and ended up at a beautiful townhouse that was even cheaper and more convenient in the Bondi Junction area.

We quickly found our groove! I jogged around the neighborhood park. Alice and Kayla went to yoga together. Keira enjoyed the spoils of the neighborhood library. Kayla, our au pair, also had ample opportunity to meet up with friends who were living in Sydney. Overall, we found our stride as a family unit.

Now that Alice and I weren't living in a campervan, we were able to bask in all that lovely Sydney had to offer. One of our favorite memories was attending an outdoor opera overlooking the Sydney Opera House. It was magical, and it would not have happened without our awesome helper, Kayla. I was so grateful to enjoy some couple's time alone with Alice. Plus Alice could have some down time to explore Sydney since I had arranged to interview nine entrepreneurs.

As in New Zealand, I arranged to talk to a diverse group of entrepreneurs. I was excited to see how welcoming they would be to share their experiences.

UNIMAIL:
From Dying to Thriving

Andrea Culligan

Harteffect (formerly The Unimail Group)

Branding and corporate communications, 50 employees, split between Australia and Canada, founded in 1999

She was once a fire breather for the Sydney Olympics. She has been a janitor and a landscaper, has stuffed envelopes and tarred roads. Yet these are still just a handful of the jobs Andrea Culligan has had. Andrea has learned that she's never too good for anything and pride doesn't get in the way of doing hard work: these lessons have served her well through life cycles and jobs, but especially as the CEO and owner of The Unimail Group (as of this writing, the company name is being changed to Harteffect, but I'll stick with what we talked about at the time of the interview).

An organization, like a civilization, can crumble from its heights, but hard choices can be made to rescue and rebuild its culture. It's not easy, but it can be done: Andrea's perseverance is a testament to that. Now, Andrea can add cultural surgeon and company cheerleader to her list of character-building jobs.

Unimail has undergone a few life cycles. When Andrea joined the company just after its inception in 1999, Unimail focused on providing emails to Australian university students, hence the name. Afterwards, Unimail diversified, creating a jobs guide for students and an online campus community. More recently, the company pivoted again, and the main thrust of the business today is corporate communications.

Leveraging its understanding of younger generations, Unimail now helps companies brand themselves in order to attract the right people at the right time with the right message. They are branding in twenty-four countries around the globe, with offices in Canada and Australia.

In 2010, Andrea Culligan was poised to exit the business due to misaligned values with her business partner. The result was Andrea's actually buying that person out, and, like with a true divorce, everyone was unhappy. This started a downward trend for Andrea and Unimail: huge disengagement, high turnover, and a pissed-off staff.

The company had accumulated two years of baggage and negativity that needed to be purged. Unlike other organizations that wallowed in and ultimately succumbed to a corrosive culture, Andrea Culligan rolled up her sleeves to rescue and redefine Unimail's personality.

Andrea shared the following insightful tactics and tips for anyone in a similar experience.

Fire Quickly

Andrea valiantly tried to change the mindset of employees, but after many attempts, she learned that some staff were mired too deeply in negativity. Either they weren't able to change or didn't want to. Andrea concluded that she was better off letting them go and bringing in much-needed new faces and attitudes.

Lead by Over-the-Top Example

As the person at the top of the pyramid, the CEO has to be clear about what the culture should look and feel like. Andrea decided to act it out in a big way: jumping on the sales desk after a big win, or saying thank you for everything to everyone constantly. She wanted to create a sense of enthusiasm and success, and she knew that it started with her.

Be Brutally Honest

She was also extremely transparent with the team. She even exclaimed to them, "We all agree this [culture] sucks. What do you guys want to do about it?"

Award Small Prizes to Ignite Discussions

During these team meetings designed to address their culture, Andrea felt frustrated that people were hesitant to speak up. To get even more involvement in the meetings, she brought small prizes, like a stationary set or funny erasers—

things she knew her team liked—in order to spur interaction and discussion. These seemingly small prizes ignited a trend of higher engagement.

Bring in an Objective Voice

It's not a sign of weakness to bring in outside, professional facilitators. In fact, these outsiders helped facilitate the crafting of a new vision and values. The outsiders' involvement democratized the process, so it never felt like Andrea was pushing the process down people's throats.

Create Values that Resonate

The vision the company originally had was not fully embraced. It was just *there*. It took them seven months to get rid of vague words like "innovation" and "happiness"—words that didn't mean much. It took time to develop them, but the new phrases really mean something in the day-to-day activities of everyone on the team.

Together, the folks at Unimail crafted the following list of values:

Explore the unfamiliar

Let there be laughter

Cultivate creativity

Think community; live green

Earn & establish respect

Do it with passion; say it with truth

Chase knowledge; share brilliance

Not only did the team identify phrases that were meaningful and personal to them, they also workshopped scenarios to practice their values, so that the culture could flourish on an ongoing basis.

> *Andrea was one of my favorite interviews and provided a wealth of invaluable tips. I like creating values that resonate, living those values, and then hiring and firing based on the values created. So many times I've seen organizations with values listed in their break room, but no one knows them, including the CEO. I'll definitely strive to bring my future company's values to life.*—David Niu

Live the Values of Which You Speak

Unimail wants to be known as "brilliant fun." "Laughter" "community" and "passion" are in their mission statement, and they drive this ethos down to their suppliers and partners. If a supplier provides a lower cost but isn't as engaging, the Unimail team will choose someone else to work with who is more fun, even if the other vendor costs more. They found that their clients were choosing Unimail not only for their work, but also for their engaging process and enjoyable interaction, so Unimail made that resonate through the supply chain, too.

Track Culture

Following another Tony Hsieh practice, Andrea tracks what employees have done to increase and improve the business culture. It's one of the seven key performance indicators that each employee is accountable for.

Hire and Fire on Values

Using Tony Hsieh's Zappo's approach, if you're not willing to hire and fire based on your organization's values, then those aren't actually values. Those are just cultural points. So get clear on what you are willing to hire and fire on, and do it. And if you're not fun … sorry, but Unimail will fire you!

Treasure Weekly 1-on-1s

Even though Andrea Culligan has a frantic travel schedule, she maintains her weekly Monday meeting with her team. During these meetings, she asks three simple questions:

1) What are you doing?

2) What happened last week and what's happening this week?

3) What are your key challenges and how can I help?

She keeps these meetings short and straightforward. This weekly rhythm also enables her to address any issues that may pop up, so nothing festers out of her sight.

Celebrate New Employees

Instead of going away parties, Andrea prefers Cameron Herold's philosophy of celebrating new employees coming onboard instead. She shared with me that on the first day, a new employee will:

- Have business cards waiting for them on their desk
- Have a laptop waiting for them on their desk with email set up and ready to go
- Receive a card and a bottle of champagne to take home and share with their significant other to celebrate their first day
- Go to lunch with the team at their favorite type of restaurant (at the end of their first week.) Everyone at the lunch shares three facts about themselves that no one would know or three facts about the person sitting next to them.

Performance Review = Praise

Andrea Culligan believes that performance reviews should always be about praise. She thinks that a manager should never wait until a yearly assessment to address any inadequacies or potential termination issues. Since she would address any red flags during her weekly 1-on-1s, problems should not fester long enough to make it to the annual review.

Reward the Actions that Help the Bottom Line

Andrea believes that 70 percent of the decisions made by Unimail employees directly affect margins. For example, these decisions could be improving prices from printers and media buyers or negotiating with freelancers for better terms. Andrea's team knows that they're able to affect the bottom line, which ultimately impacts their bonus. She has created an effective system of ownership where employees treat the business as if it were their own.

Offer a Choice of Bonus

When people go above and beyond and have earned a bonus, Andrea gives them a choice between cash or a gift. Most employees take the cash, but Andrea prefers to give a gift because it's much more memorable. For example, one employee got the iPad 3 the day it was released. Another employee received a nursing chair.

Staying in Touch With a Monthly Newsletter

At fifty employees between two offices in different countries, not everyone knows about each other's projects. Unimail created a monthly newsletter, which has been a hit and a fantastic tool for knowledge-sharing and internal recognition.

Honor the Employee of the Month

Once a month, everyone votes for the Employee of the Month, who gets a half-day off, a massive sombrero, and their picture in the newsletter.

Cherish Employees

To accommodate new moms and help keep them at work, Unimail is redesigning a conference room into a childcare area. To work around regulations, parents are in charge of hiring the caretaker.

Conclusion

It wasn't easy, and only two out of fourteen original employees are left after fourteen months of reshaping Unimail. Walking around the offices, I could feel the positive energy and a sense that everyone truly enjoyed their roles. And Andrea isn't resting on her laurels. Instead, she continuously seeks ways to improve their culture. Because, as we all know, it's much easier to maintain a trajectory rather than to reverse it. And Unimail's culture is definitely aimed at a bright, bright future.

BODY BOLSTER:
Healthy Business

Flavia Abbate

CityClinic & **Body Bolster**

A one-stop physical therapy shop and distributor of physical therapy tools, 44 employees, founded in 1998

Flavia Abbate's road to entrepreneurialism started when a consulting client asked her to create an executive health module for their business. The client wanted not just marketing communication that promoted health, but an actual program. Flavia collaborated with her identical twin sister's husband, who happened to be a trainer to Mr. Universe, and they hit on a great formula. After the success of this first module, they rolled out other similar programs to other clients. The modules were so successful that in 1998, they started the first CityClinic. They wanted executives to have a dedicated physical space to learn more and get specialized health services.

CityClinic offered a revolutionary approach by housing all experts under one roof—from physiotherapists to osteopaths to chiropractors. People in the industry thought they were nuts, since these disciplines tend to compete with each other. But to Flavia Abbate, the merging seemed like a natural approach: it's more patient-centric to house all of these options in one centralized location.

Five years after the success of CityClinic, Flavia and her team bought the assets for BodyBolster. Everyone at CityClinic was already a fan of this dowdy, grey physical therapy tool. So, on a tentative impulse, they tossed in a bid, never thinking that they would win. Next thing they knew, though, they owned BodyBolster. Flavia and the team spent the next eighteen months repositioning the foam roller (a device for stretching and muscle support) to make it more marketable, and it quickly became popular in both the rehab and general marketplaces.

Today, CityClinic and BodyBolster combined employ forty-four people. The culture of both companies has stayed intact and smooth through the transitions over the years. Flavia attributes this cohesion to the entire staff having a personal interest in wellness. Almost all of the employees came to work there via word-of-mouth because they were drawn to the business. The glue between the team and the business is a deep interest in health for themselves, their community, and their clients—but they also have a lot of fun stretching and rolling on the floor together with the bolsters.

Flavia Abbate shared the following lessons to help fellow entrepreneurs and business owners.

Create an Open Familial Culture

Earlier in her life, Flavia had worked in a warm, nurturing ambiance cultivated by the owner of a publishing firm. Feeling like one of the family, Flavia believed that they could achieve anything while working there. The owner gave his team leeway to do and create beyond normal boundaries and to distinguish themselves and try new things. Everyone put in extra hours because they all felt part of something special towards which they could make a concrete contribution. This experience inspired Flavia to strive for the same type of culture at CityClinic and BodyBolster.

Flavia relates to her team like real family members and has a very encouraging style. She connects with the team's shared passion for the product and wellness for all. She doesn't feel that they are working *for* her—she feels that she is doing this business *along with* them. Rolling up her sleeves or getting down on the ground to stretch is part of what makes them comfortable with her, and in turn, her enthusiasm rubs off on them.

Rally Around a Greater Purpose

The health crisis and the mission to make people healthier drives Flavia and everyone who works with her. I learned from Flavia that Australia possesses an obesity problem. To combat this, CityClinic just acquired one of the first new Body Composition Analysis Technology machines. This machine measures visceral fat deposits around the heart, liver, and kidneys. In addition, you can get extremely accurate body-fat percentage measurements without being dunked into a tub of water the old-fashioned way.

Flavia states that children as young as fifteen have musculoskeletal problems seen previously only in adults. This deeply concerns her, and she wants to raise awareness and tackle the issue. "It's meaningful and important to me," she asserted. When a company's mission is about saving lives, it's not hard to find enthusiastic people to sign on to your cause.

Recruit Product Users for Employees

Amazingly, all six of the employees at BodyBolster used the product before they worked there. I can't think of any other organization with such a high ratio of groupies! In fact, Flavia spends exactly $0 in HR recruiting for BodyBolster. People specifically seek out openings at her company. To all business owners out there—how much do *your* customers and employees love your offering?

Offer an Emotional Sales Proposition

The BodyBolster product resonates strongly with its users on an emotional level. They love it, identify with it, and associate it with being healthy and active. It has kind of a cult following, and this emotional attachment has been a strong asset that will carry the brand for years to come.

Outsource Data Collection for Reviews

To prepare for her annual reviews, Flavia Abbate outsources to an HR person. This individual collects and collates information for the direct reports whom she'll review. Flavia has the luxury of outsourcing this task because the executive team takes careful notes during their monthly company performance reviews. These monthly reviews are then collected and rolled up for the annual January review, and no one is caught cramming to prepare days before the big assessment.

Ask These Three Questions Each Day

At the end of each day, Flavia and her partners ask their staff three quick questions.

- What have you achieved today that was good?
- What would you like to do better?
- What was your enjoyment level today? They rate the enjoyment level on a scale of 1-5.

This helps Flavia quickly catch and address any issues before they fester.

Having a daily check-in is such a great idea. I typically do a standing huddle in the morning, but it also seems to work at the end of the day. Her three questions are also great to uncover progress, improvement opportunities, and a pulse on how happy each staff member is. —David Niu

---

Conclusion

Flavia and the team rally around the mission of health and fitness, which becomes the glue in the culture that keeps them inspired and motivated. She also lives and builds on the culture by holding many staff meetings with everyone in gym clothes, on the ground, and using their BodyBolsters to stretch, tone, and try out new exercises. I don't think they'll be training the next Mr. Universe anytime soon, but they're definitely building more fans by creating healthier habits for their clients and community.

WEDDING LIST CO:
I Dos and Business Don'ts

George & Karaline Loiterton

Wedding List Co

Leading service provider for
wedding registries in Australia, 25
Employees, founded in 2003

It happens: people get married and have a negative experience with their online wedding registry. They do not, however, usually start up a company to address the problem. George and Karaline Loiterton started Wedding List Co in 2003 to do just that. The couple had been working in London and got married in Tuscany. They set up one bridal registry for their UK guests and another one for their Australian people, and were quickly dismayed by the limited and poor offerings and lackluster customer service available in the Australian registry compared to the robust UK registry options.

The Loitertons planned to return to Australia and debated whether to get full-time jobs or start a business that might afford some freedom when they started a family. Initially, they looked into the wedding registry landscape, thinking the idea was so obvious that others must have tried it and failed due to some marketplace limitation. As fate would have it, that was not the case. So, eager to start their lives together for richer or poorer, they opted to build their own business, and Wedding List Co was born.

Wedding List Co is now Australia's leading service provider for bridal registries. They focus on great service, unique brands, and an optimal experience for both wedding couples and wedding guests. Wedding List Co employs twenty-five staff now. A few things that distinguish their service:

- **Website**—the Wedding List Co's website offers the ability to make online purchases, a feature that the major retailers in Australia currently do not offer. This is a massive competitive advantage.
- **Store/Brand**—the Wedding List Co store at Bondi Junction is airy, intimate, and inviting. They carry a selection of great brands—some of which are exclusive to them (there are also showrooms in Melbourne, Brisbane, and Perth).
- **Team/Customer Service**—George Loiterton always receives positive comments on his team, especially compared to larger department stores' service.

George is very truthful about how much hard work has gone into growing his own company. The dream of owning your own business always embraces flexibility, self-direction, and high returns. The reality, however, also includes very long hours, unexpected business curve balls, sole accountability, and risk.

Typical with a company at this size, Wedding List Co does not have a human resource department. George focuses mainly on business issues, and not so much on motivating the team. But along the way, he has developed and adopted effective management techniques to keep his employees engaged.

Here are some insights that's he learned during his past nine years at Wedding List Co.

Creating a Culture of Trust

Striving to reflect his own values and what he wants in his life, George has tried to create a culture of trust and accountability. He likes giving employees the latitude to try new things and learn from mistakes. But on the flipside, he has employed some people who respect only the "rights" part of the equation, not their responsibility to the company. Naturally, he tries to weed out those folks. As George begins to trust workers with more flexibility, he shares with them his vision of responsibility and what that entails.

Daily 9:09 Huddle

To improve communications, George holds daily team meetings at 9:09 every morning. He adopted this idea from Verne Harnish, the founder of EO and the author of *Mastering the Rockefeller Habits*. He chose a "unique" starting time to help make it easy to remember when the huddle begins. Furthermore, to make sure people get there on time, the last person who arrives speaks first. Everyone hears what's going on with the company and what everyone else is working on. George also gets a quick pulse on everyone's mood. I would highly recommend the book since I also implement techniques from it, too.

Leverage Job Description in Reviews

George Loiterton admits annual appraisals can be awkward conversations. To ease the awkwardness, he leverages the reviewee's job description and uses that as a template for the review. Since both parties have agreed to the job description upon hiring or when someone's role has changed, using the job-spec template helps depolarize the conversation and provide structure.

Love/Loathe Exercises

George performs these exercises once every six months. He gives each employee a week to think about the tasks that they love and loathe to do at Wedding List Co. He then reviews the list with each person, and he's honest about whether or not it includes things that he can help with or change. These reports provide great insight into motivations and areas that do and don't excite the staff. The process also offers employees a healthy, non-confrontational communication platform.

> *I agree that this is a thought-provoking and non-confrontational way to discover what motivates and demotivates the team. I also appreciate how George acknowledges when he can't do something to help someone. At least that person knows that George is listening; George closes the loop by validating their feedback.*—David Niu

Hands-on conflict resolution

George often jumps in to put together small, ad hoc "working teams" to hammer through a specific problem, and sometimes he pulls people aside to work out communications hiccups or training needs.

Conclusion

George and Karaline Loiterton have created an amazing bricks-and-mortar-plus-online business over the past nine years. They jumped in feet first and built what they themselves wanted as well as what they thought the broader market needed, too. Today, customers love the staff at Wedding List Co.; George cited people as one of the company's top three strategic assets. But at the same time, George admitted that he currently focuses more on pressing company issues than he does on his people. But right after our discussion, he was inspired to set up meetings for the next round of Love/Loathe exercises. It's a good reminder for all managers: think about how much time is devoted to working *in* the business versus working *on* the business.

THE HALLWAY:
Sailing and Prevailing

Jules Hall

The Hallway

Brand-building advertising agency, 25 employees, founded in 2007

Jules Hall's first job was driving a tractor around and around his family's farm. From that experience, he learned that he hated getting paid a fixed wage for fixed work—he knew there had to be a better way. So, when Jules reached university, he got his creative juices flowing and started Jules Hall Productions, selling t-shirts at the local pub. It was ingenuity at its best because Jules could 1) drink pints with his mates while "working," 2) meet women at the pub, and 3) make money by peddling his shirts. His all-time best selling t-shirt was emblazoned with the slogan, "If all else fails, excess prevails!"

After graduating from college (and from selling t-shirts), Jules took a turn at Andersen Consulting, and then joined one of the first digital agencies in London. The emerging digital media held exciting potential that stimulated Jules' creativity, and the startup environment suited his adventurous spirit.

Eventually, Jules ended up as GM of a premier agency in Sydney. Being somewhat of a maverick, he started envisioning a new type of advertising business. Not wanting to be the digital equivalent of a bricklayer that performs only one function, Jules designed an agency that would combine the spectrum of elements needed to build brands for companies: an agency that would more be more of a "communications architect" than a specialized "builder."

With that inspiration, Jules launched The Hallway in 2007 with a laptop and a borrowed office. They are continuously growing, but staying true to Jules' original mission: developing creative ideas using a combination of advertising and content, PR, design, branding and technology.

Jules relayed The Hallway's three main strategic assets:

- Communication Architecture Methodology—this is the priority framework, developed and fine-tuned to answer all briefs.
- People—The Hallway has been very diligent in hiring people who are thorough and passionate about creating absolutely the best work for their clients.
- Culture—Jules describes their culture as rigorous and intellectually ambitious. People challenge and question assumptions and ideas during meetings. Jules admits that this can be intimidating to some people, but he and the staff thrive in this type of environment and know that it's borne from the passion of people sharing the singular goal of creating not just the best

solution for clients, but also work that will be recognized for global innovation.

The Hallway's success has not flown under the radar: the company has been rated one of the "Hottest Agencies" in Sydney, according to Agency Creative/Billings Index 2012. Jules discussed what he's learned over the last four years in order to get The Hallway to where it is today.

"Continue | Start | Stop" Review Format

Jules Hall keeps the performance reviews simple at The Hallway, with a one-page-style review format. Under each bucket, he'll put three to four bulleted examples: Continue—what you are doing that is great; Start—I want you to do (x); and Stop—what is not working. This becomes the focal point for each person during reviews and catch-ups, making their discussion succinct and easy to remember.

> *Similar to George Loiterton's Love and Loathe exercise, I find Jules' Continue, Start, Stop to be highly engaging and effective. In fact, I've used this in the past and really enjoyed the outcome. It's also a great exercise to break out as teams in quarterly company meetings to see what employees think. The responses that are particularly noteworthy are usually the "Stop" comments.*—David Niu

Keep a Little Black Book

Like most managers, Jules finds it difficult to keep on top of feedback with concrete examples. His tip is to write down staff wins and areas for improvement in the back pages of his black notebook. He always has ample examples with details to draw from when it comes time for performance reviews.

Overhire for Key Roles

Jules freely admits that they just massively overinvested by hiring a Head of Operations. Yet he realized that for The Hallway to succeed as an agency, stronger processes and methodologies were needed to liberate creativity. It's a bold bet by Jules to understand the main leverage points for growth and then to invest in it ahead of the curve.

Careful to "Not Do Business with Yourself"

At the beginning, Jules spent countless hours analyzing and reviewing spreadsheets and other business data points. He loved to dive into data. But his mentor questioned the value of so much analysis, and reminded Jules of The Hallway's aim. His mentor basically said, "Sell some work and make some money." It was a good reminder of the basics. If it works, then just carry on.

Embrace People Management

Jules admits that he used to fear people-management. But now it's exciting and extremely rewarding when he gets it right. I think he realizes that as a manager, you are leading people on a journey, not just to a destination. And since every entrepreneur has a journey, why not have a positive attitude about it and smell as many roses along the way as possible?

Conclusion

Jules has successfully grown The Hallway from an idea over lunch to an industry award-winner. Along the way, he's embraced teachings from his childhood, mentors and business experience. He's created a rigorous work environment in order to get the best out of his people, and he's designed a culture that hires for and supports this approach.

Jules Hall definitely has the presence of a thoughtful, intelligent leader with a personality that fills a room, yet at the same time he's got a laid-back charm. I found him humble, self-effacing, and funny. He's come a long way from designing "daggy" (Aussie slang for unstylish but comfy) t-shirts, and the future looks promising from down The Hallway.

PUREPROFILE:
Clever Culture

Paul Chan

Pureprofile

Web-based consumer purchasing survey and rewards service, 67 employees, founded in 2007

Paul Chan's father was an entrepreneur, so it's no surprise that Paul's first job was in the family business. At thirteen years old, Paul worked at his father's Yum Cha restaurant in Sydney's Chinatown and quickly learned that work could be hard—not necessarily because of the physical aspect or the environment, but because a job is something that you have to wake up and do *every day*. So hopefully your job is something you can be passionate about. Going beyond even being passionate, Paul decided that he wanted to innovate and redefine traditional ways of working.

Paul studied land economics at University of Technology in Sydney, and while working in the Silicon Valley on real estate marketing projects, the Internet boom grabbed Paul's fascination. What really compelled him was the Internet's power as a two-way communication tool taken to a very broad level while enabling access to very deep data. He planned to focus on the Internet's depth rather than its broadcast capabilities, which was what many consumer-based Internet companies focused on at the time. But one day the phrase "capturing eyeballs" became common parlance.

In 2000, Paul Chan followed his own passion to start Pureprofile. Consumers use this web-based service as "account holders," building their own extensive profile around likes, dislikes, their purchasing decisions, and demographics. Account holders are carefully segmented according to their answers; this allows businesses, researchers, academics, and marketers to offer their services or products efficiently to the right people. Using complex methodologies and consumers' full participation in research and surveys, the exchange between customer and business is very "pure," hence the name of the company. Today, Pureprofile employs sixty-seven people across five offices (Sydney, Mumbai, London, New York, and San Francisco). It's one of the top survey sites with over a million users and hundreds of clients.

Over the years, Paul has taken pains to build his company completely by his own design: the technology, culture, systems, and environment are his own. Maybe it's the nature of an Internet entrepreneur to be so independent, or perhaps Paul's early experience in the restaurant drove him to create a career on his own terms.

Paul has a very analytical personality that thrives on efficiency and self-sufficiency. This permeates Pureprofile's company, down to the last hire. Pureprofile has an extremely independent and self-managed culture (the buck stops with you). This allows Paul to think "big-picture" and not worry about the day-to-day operations.

Mirroring Paul's passion for efficiency is the technology itself. The company has built an amazingly complex and efficient system to manage millions of profiles and enable correct payment to the users who respond to the surveys. In addition, this platform also matches the correct users with businesses that need their feedback.

Efficiency and productivity are hard enough to manage in one office, but connecting five locations around the world has taken some effort. Through clever technology, they've been able to connect the offices together as they work around-the-clock. They're able to share their information, updates, and culture seamlessly.

To build such a successful business, Paul Chan admits that he's "not afraid to lose." Along that same vein, Paul shares some of his losses and lessons as he's built Pureprofile.

Design Everything

When starting Pureprofile, Paul realized that he possessed a unique opportunity to purposefully design everything. He took time to think everything through and implement his vision early on. It's definitely much easier to be proactive at the blueprint phase than after the foundation has been set and the frame has been erected. Staying true to this commitment, Paul has thrown out old review formats and is designing his own program to streamline the process.

Take Caution when Hiring Senior People from Large Companies

Paul Chan found that oftentimes, hiring senior people from big corporations is high risk for a startup. Most executives who work at large organizations have a full complement of support staff and a budget. When they're removed from that environment and dropped into a scrappy start-up, they often struggle without the resources that they are accustomed to leveraging.

> *This tip really resonates with me because we initially brought in a new CEO for NetConversions, only to have to let him go months later. Similar to Paul, I now ask how executives will execute against an agreed upon plan. At a startup phase, they usually have to be a player first, then a coach. When formulating an execution plan, if their first question is "How much budget do I have?" or "What agency can I hire?" then alarm bells go off for me. They have to be able to roll up their sleeves and get sh*t done themselves. Then as we grow, they can start coaching others when we build out the team.* —David Niu

Keep Expectations High for High Level Employees

Paul is confident in himself and his role, so he gives people a lot of responsibility and helps develop confidence in others. He acknowledges that in some cases this leads to over-promoting people, pushing them beyond their comfort level. But this is how he has built his culture of accountability and productivity. He feels that when you push people at a high level, the low-level day-to-day processes get taken care of automatically. Additionally, Paul is an early adapter of tools to help people get the job done.

Communicate With Trust

Many entrepreneurs who don't code or read programming languages struggle with measuring the performance of developers. Paul engages constantly with his technical people to hear their opinion on the code. They give him accurate responses because he has created a culture where people can speak honestly. They might say, "It's not that good" or "It's working but I'd like to fix it" or, hopefully, "It's really good code!"

Procure Mentor Feedback

Paul is quite conscientious when it comes to getting feedback to improve his own performance. He invests regular time into deep discussions with his team. On top of that, he has a mentor who works weekly with him and his senior team. He values having a continuous feedback loop so that he can adjust course quickly when necessary and keep a steady momentum going.

Do Something With The Data You Collect

Paul is maniacal about measuring, monitoring, and diving into data, which is a great fit for Pureprofile's business model. He shared with me that most companies have a huge amount of data that is never processed into information—much less knowledge or wisdom.

Love What You Do

This obviously sounds trite, but Paul has witnessed too many entrepreneurs who aren't truly passionate about what they do. This is surprising since one would think that people tend to start companies that they're passionate about. Entrepreneurs pour endless hours into their startups, so you should spend your energy on something that you're passionate about, or start thinking about how to transition and exit from that endeavor.

Conclusion

At an early age, Paul Chan realized what he didn't want to do. But it was only later that he was able to combine his passion for data and creating systems into Pureprofile. Paul is definitely very intentional about designing and guiding his business, as I saw from their swanky office location and furnishings. It's easy to choose to be great, but it's much more difficult to follow through like Paul Chan has at Pureprofile.

THE NILE:
The River Delivers

Jethro Marks

The Nile

Online store for books, DVDs, and more, 40 employees, founded 2003

Jethro Marks had just returned to New Zealand after a nine-month backpacking trip through South America and decided that he needed either to get a job or start a business. He chose the latter, and rounded up two good mates to try their hand at selling goods online. They experimented with selling books, CDs, DVDs, games, sheepskin products, Maori artwork, high-end jewelry, low-end jewelry, and even Polynesian cots.

After six months, they were in twelve different product categories, but the only consistently productive one was books. Customers ordering a book knew exactly what they would receive, unlike a diamond purchase, which requires lots of specification and a long sales cycle. Book sales had lower margins, but returns and customer demands were also low, and the sales process was straightforward.

So they decided to focus on books and build a business around it.

Before diving in, they needed to come up with a company name. Anyone who has tried to start a business knows that this isn't the easiest thing to do. They went back and forth for three months and tossed around names using a river theme. "The Murray" (Australia's longest river) didn't quite fit; they thought "Yangtze" was too difficult to spell. Realizing that the Nile was actually longer than the Amazon, they made their pick. In 2003, they officially launched TheNile.com.au.

Almost a decade later, The Nile employs forty people with offices in Auckland and Sydney. The company found success as an online store for books, CDs, and DVDs, but other departments have recently been rolled out, such as health and beauty, baby, sports, wine, and others. The Nile offers Australians and New Zealanders the entire range of products that consumers could buy overseas, but from a local company in local currency with competitive or better pricing and local customer service.

Jethro Marks shares the following ups and downs from his experience in growing TheNile.com.au to the successful organization that it is today.

Engineering the Course of a Culture

The Nile was the first organization that I spoke with that does not have a written set of cultural values. And it's not because the management team doesn't care about culture— just that culture had not been enough of an issue in employee engagement or staff retention to motivate the team to sit down and crystallize their values. Furthermore, offices split between Auckland and Sydney have each developed independent, different cultures on their own. Jethro views the two offices' customs as being irreconcilable, having totally different styles.

He admits that he'd prefer better alignment across the two offices and among the three types of staff: developers, back office, and warehouse. He wants everyone to be 100 percent bought-in and passionate about the company's mission: delivering goods to customers.

Deliver on Promise to Customers

From day one, Jethro reiterated to everyone in the company that they must deliver on their promise to customers: it was their most important job. During Christmas season, he personally leads the charge, with the entire company swamping the warehouse to ensure that packages get out on time. Jethro acknowledges that this passion to please the customer is the core of his values, and that it leads everything else at the Nile. How it gets done is considered secondary.

Emulating the Best Examples of Different Companies

Jethro has definitely followed the success of Zappos and their competition with Amazon (before Amazon acquired Zappos). On the one hand, Zappos' 1-800 number is located prominently on the homepage above the fold. On the other hand, Amazon tries to use as much automation as possible, and it's very difficult to reach a live person in real time there.

Even though these companies take different approaches to customer service, they have proven each approach can be successful. Jethro decided to leverage the best of both companies. He focuses on automation and providing a great customer experience. At the same time, if a customer needs support, he displays his phone number right on the homepage too.

Jethro also shared an experience comparing two companies' customer service approaches. He sent identical emails to Zappos and Mavi, looking to find a pair of Mavi jeans. He wrote:

```
>—-customer message to follow—-
>Hello
>I'm after this product:
>http://www.zappos.com/mavi-jeans-josh-
low-rise-easy-bootcut-in-rinse-american-
vintage
>My size is 34/30
>The Mavi code is 00 450 7779
>Are you able to source this item for
me?
>Thanks
>Jethro
```

The following response is from Mavi, who replied right away:

Dear Jethro,

Thank you for contacting us! We typically replenish our inventory every 2 to 3 weeks. We recommend continually checking our website for availability or sign up for "can't find your size." As soon as the item is replenished, you will receive an email notification. If you have any further questions, please give us a call. Thank you and have a wonderful day!

Kind Regards,

Customer Service

Mavi USA Online

customerservice@shopmavi.us   (mailto: customerservice@shopmavi.us)

1-866-525-1631 Phone
310-868-2938 Fax

http://www.shopmavi.us

****

He was not impressed with Mavi's response, but it was received same day. But then he got Zappos' response the next day:

Hello Jethro,
Thank you for contacting the Zappos Customer Loyalty Team. I hope you're having a beautiful day so far. My name is Courtney and I'm here to assist you today!
Unfortunately, it does not look like we will be carrying the Mavi Jeans Josh Low Rise Easy Bootcut in Rinse American Vintage jeans in your size as it is

currently out of stock on our website and we do not have any open purchase orders with the manufacturer. I'm very sorry. I did browse competitor sites to see if I could find the jeans but it's my best guess that this item has been discontinued as I could not locate it anywhere. You are always welcome to contact the manufacturer as they would have more information as to whether or not the item has been discontinued and if not, where you may be able to purchase it. I'm sorry I wasn't able to help any further.

Thanks again for contacting us here at Zappos.com. If you have any further questions, please don't hesitate to ask, we are here 24/7 via phone, Live Chat and Email. Have a wonderful day, Jethro!

Yours in service,

Courtney S.

Zappos.com

Powered by Service!

Phone: Toll-free 1-800-ZAPPOS-1 (1-800-927-7677

e-mail: cs@zappos.com

http://www.zappos.com

****

Jethro was thoroughly impressed with the thorough, thoughtful response from Zappos, especially since they weren't even the manufacturer of the jeans. Just reading the two, you can clearly see how much more enthusiastic, empathetic, and personal (including the employee's name) the Zappos' response is.

Review More than Metrics

When I asked Jethro about the assessment process at The Nile, Jethro made it clear that their reviews have been designed to stimulate a dialogue about how the employee feels about their performance and about the company. In the past, they used a 1 to 5 scale, and he noticed that this numerical rating approach dampened these meetings. Conversations would get pigeonholed into a numerical ranking of specific skills and weren't achieving the outcome he was seeking, such as whether someone has the proper tools to succeed or the employee's career path at the company.

So, in October of last year, he switched to an entirely qualitative-based annual appraisal form. Thus far, he's been pleased with the increase in dialogue and conversation, which is the goal for him during the review. He still doesn't think that he perfected a way to map key performance indicators in a way that would drive a compensation increase, so he will still seek out an improved system.

Find Someone to Guide the Co-founders' Reviews

In addition to Jethro Marks, there are two other co-founders. They talk all the time and discuss issues often, but they've never dug deeply enough to review the performance of one another. Jethro decided to hire an outside facilitator to conduct a three- to four-hour management review session.

The three co-founders didn't have to prepare, nor did the facilitator have any background on them or the company. Instead, she just dove in and asked pointed questions such as,

"What should this person do more of? What should this person do less of? What should this person stop doing?" The session definitely exceeded his expectations, and he recommends this approach to other business leaders.

> *I know it's difficult for people at the top of the pyramid to get honest feedback from their subordinates. So I think it's a great idea to bring in an unbiased outsider to help compile feedback from the team and deliver the themes to the executives.*—David Niu

Conclusion

Being from Seattle (Amazon country), I had looked forward to interviewing Jethro and learning about his company's growth. Jethro proved that there's not just one path to success. For example, Zappos adopts a high-touch customer approach, Amazon takes a low-touch customer approach, and the Nile.com.au leverages a customer approach in between the two.

As The Nile continues to grow and maintain two separate office locations with different cultures, it'll be interesting to follow the company's development and how they attempt to create a more singular culture around which everyone can rally.

POSSE:
Rocking Reality

Rebekah Campbell

Posse

A social search engine for sharing and discovering fun places, 13 Employees, founded in 2010

Rebekah Campbell of Posse is a natural self-starter and promoter.

At thirteen, Rebekah attended a birthday party at a local restaurant and was bored by the clown that was entertaining the guests. The very next day, Rebekah called the restaurant owner and sold him on reasons why she should be the new clown. She was hired instantly and loved her job—she even joined the union (who knew there was one?) From this experience, she learned the power of asking. If you don't take initiative and ask, you won't ever get.

Even before that, at age seven, Rebekah had learned a valuable lesson about work. Selling flowers from her house, she couldn't get cars to stop by, and she did not make a single sale. The next day, her mother bought her some balloons to make her stand more noticeable. After Rebekah had sold all her flowers that afternoon, she burst into the house to tell her mom. Rebekah was calmly and quickly given a bill for the balloon investment. Business has costs before it has profitability at any stage—or age.

As an adult, Rebekah landed in the music industry as a concert promoter. She started her own music management company and got creative selling the tour for the well-known Australian rock band Evermore. Rebekah maintained tight budgets when promoting concerts, usually spending around $20,000 to put up posters and advertise in music publications. She could quickly tell if the campaign was working based on how ticket sales in the first few days.

Unfortunately, for an Evermore concert in Perth, her methods were not working. Rebekah devised another plan and emailed the passionate fans of Evermore in Perth, offering them the opportunity to promote the show. She allotted participants tickets to sell in exchange for a commission and even benefits for selling more, like gaining better seats for themselves. Lo and behold, she ended up selling out Perth and went on to be very successful in concert promotion.

After several fruitful years in this field, Rebekah Campbell decided to start a technology company to capitalize on her inspiration. Posse, founded in 2010, started out as a digital music promotion service but has since transitioned into a broader sector. Posse has evolved into a social search engine that gets people excited to share their favorite places with friends and receive recommendations about experiences from others. The company employs thirteen people, and Rebekah relates below the wins and re-dos from starting Posse.

Caution when Outsourcing Development

Since Rebekah cannot write code, she outsourced Posse's early-stage development to India. She quickly learned one of the main drawbacks of this approach was that the outsourced developers weren't obsessing about the service. They were just writing the code according to the specifications. But even when coding to specifications, there are tons of mini-decisions that need to be made along the way. And if the developer is not invested in solving the customer's problem, the decisions won't be optimized around that.

Rebekah concedes that it may make more sense to outsource development if the prototype or code is straightforward. But what they were developing at Posse was just too dynamic and innovative for an outsourced solution to work for them.

Trust Your Vision

On the other hand, if you're the founder but cannot code, ceding the vision to a technical team can challenge your confidence in how the product should work if someone tells you "it can't be done." But Rebekah conceived the concept, stuck to it, and found a team that could make it happen exactly the way she wanted it to.

Hire Slowly

It took Rebekah quite a while to find the right CTO, but she thinks that finding her current guy, Alex North, to fill the role is the best thing that has happened to Posse. She's also relieved that she didn't jump the gun and hire someone who wasn't right for such a key position. With a small team, Rebekah willingly sacrificed rapid growth to find the right team member.

Fire Fast

Rebekah Campbell admits that they are ruthless at Posse when a new hire doesn't fit in. In fact, they let someone go who was a good coder but did not embrace their culture within the first two weeks. Now, whenever she gets a gut feeling, she knows that she needs to act on it—posthaste.

Harder Interviews

After spending a good amount of time to find Alex North for the lead technical role, Posse revamped its interview process. Rebekah admits that she likes people and wants applicants to do well, but previously she didn't screen as stringently as she should have. Now she's much more skeptical and tougher, and she even conducts exercises with the applicants. They'll usually hold at least three interviews, if not five, before making a decision. In addition, she now looks for the holes in the applicant rather than for the good spots. She notes that this is much tougher, but the results speak for themselves—they have a much stronger team today.

> I'm a believer of the adage "hire slow and fire quick." If someone doesn't fit with our organization, then we're doing them a disservice to keep them languishing. I opt for transparency and coaching to course-correct quickly for these individuals. I believe it's fair to all parties. The time that leaders invest in problematic employees is time that _should_ be investing in the stars. Stars drive our business!
>
> I think Jack Welch once suggested taking out a piece of paper and writing down all the names of your direct reports. By their name, write what percentage of your mentoring and coaching time goes to each one. Then rank who is the most valuable to your organization. Many managers spend the majority of their coaching time with the laggards instead of focusing on stars. Firing quickly enables more time investment in stars. And since firing is a painful process, it also serves to continually improve the hiring process to ensure we bring on the right folks in the first place.—David Niu

Quarterly Performance Review Cycles

Posse leverages a lot of the best practices from Google (where Alex used to work), including the quarterly performance-review cycles. During these quarterly performance reviews, everyone writes down their contributions and concerns for that quarter. Rebekah really likes this approach because everyone is always thinking about what they're going to be able to list under contributions, and they can focus on working towards that.

Emphasize Strengths and Don't Obsess Over Weaknesses

Alex, Posse's CTO, likes to focus on individual's strengths and leverage those instead of trying to improve his employees' weaknesses. This perspective sounds like the missive that Marcus Buckingham delivers in his book _Now, Discover Your Strengths_. At Posse, they eschew detailed action plans that focus on how to round out an employee's weaknesses and instead plan around how to focus on something at which they excel.

Spread Ownership

Everyone at Posse receives stock options so that they gain a sense of ownership. In addition, Rebekah tries to be as inclusive as possible when it comes to strategic planning and brainstorming. She admits that this method is more challenging, but she thinks it's worthwhile if everyone buys in.

Leader Transparency to Set Tone for Reviews

Rebekah also shares with her management team her own quarterly contributions and company concerns. She always speaks first in these meetings and finds that the more open and vulnerable she is, the deeper the team digs to truly get to the heart of issues. To see how much she actually walks the talk about transparency, go to her blog to learn about the ups and downs of her journey developing and growing Posse at: www.rebekahcampbell.com.

Conclusion

From selling flowers to being a clown to promoting bands to starting Posse, Rebekah learned some critical lessons on being a better leader and embracing change.

She figures that entrepreneurs fear failure less than they fear missing out. Which is probably part of the reason why she couldn't buy a house; instead, she used the down payment that she had saved for a home to purchase the

Posse.com domain name after a fierce back-and-forth in an online auction.

Similarly, Rebekah shared that at her most recent staff Christmas party, she looked in stunned silence around the table at the eleven people who attended. She realized that none of the people from the previous year's Christmas party were there, including her board members—the company had seen a complete 100 percent turnover rate in only a year. Trusting in her vision means not missing out on seeing all that Posse can become.

KOSKELA:
Grab a Chair and Stay a While

Sasha Titchkosky

Koskela

Designing and creating high quality furniture, 14 employees, founded in 2000

Sasha Titchkosky's first job was working at a shop that sold all things related to Manchester. In fact, she had to take over the entire store when the owner went on vacation shortly after she started. He called her after the first day of his vacation to see how sales went. He was shocked to find out that sixteen-year-old Sasha had sold more merchandise in one day than he'd sold the entire previous week. From this early experience, Sasha learned the importance of talking to and engaging with customers.

In her formal career after university, Sasha worked at a few large corporations but then became jaded. She felt uninspired, navigating her work life without mentors or passion. Her husband was in the same boat, eager to make a change. Sasha surveyed the Australian furniture market and identified a gap for midmarket products that were designed and produced in Australia. So in 2000, with her husband, Russell, they founded Koskela.

In the corporate world, Sasha had witnessed a tremendous waste of office furnishings. Companies that would do a fit-out would just cycle through another remodel in five years, whether or not the furniture was outdated or undamaged.

Hence Sasha makes a point at Koskela to focus on creating high-quality, enduring pieces that can be reused as much as possible (for example, re-upholstered). They have a take-back policy at the end of a piece's cycle, so they may strip a returned piece to its components and refurbish it for reuse.

Furthermore, Koskela collaborates with artisans and manufacturers in Australia and is viewed by clients as having a high level of ethics along with a passion for creating well-designed pieces. These mutually beneficial partnerships open up new markets for the parties involved and help keep the whole process local.

Today, Koskela employs eight full-time and six part-time staff. The organization pursues a culture of social ambition and conscience. Their motto is, "Follow your heart, trust your judgment, and do it with joy." The company's culture resonates so well with people that when they are looking for new staff members, they post their vacancies only on the Koskela blog and Facebook page. Sasha was shocked by the flood of applicants who applied with emotive phrases like, "I love your products. I would love to work in your store." Sasha thinks that their brand and beautiful products are strong draws for potential employees.

After eleven years, Koskela recently moved into a stunning new retail space, complete with artist space and a fabulously chic cafe. Given the organization's growth and expansion into a much larger space, Sasha shared the following experiences for other entrepreneurs to learn from.

Keep True to and Leverage Your Brand

Most other competitors in her market are just reselling an imported brand. There are very few competing firms that design and produce their own products. This commitment is something that they promote and honor, which attracts clients and employees to Koskela.

Cultural Tune-up after Major Company Milestones

After years of growth and planning for their new showroom, Sasha realized that the processes and culture they'd had when they were smaller needed to be evaluated and updated. For example, today there's too much criticism that lacks a constructive angle—some employees voice the negative side without providing any solutions. Sasha realizes that she needs to engage these people and assess how to get her culture back on the right track, since the company has grown and changed. The challenge is finding the time.

The Impact of Office Environment

Sasha sees large companies investing in their office environment all the time. However, she thinks that smaller companies don't realize how critical an office environment can be to morale and company image. The kicker: they don't have to spend huge amounts of money to improve their office environment.

I admit it—I'm cheap, especially when it comes to office aesthetics. But I have converted to investing in an engaging workplace. I want to create a workplace where I feel excited to spend long hours and that I'm proud to showcase to candidates, clients, and my parents quite frankly.

Like our careercation, it doesn't have to cost an arm and a leg. Lifehacker.com and other sites detail how Ikea can be cheap chic. And it's pretty fun trying to design an office on a shoestring because we all have to get creative.—David Niu

---

Conclusion

While enjoying a bite from the yummy cafe during our interview, Sasha remarked that she really admires how well-run and efficient the cafe's operations are. Everyone has a well-defined role within a structured hierarchy and executes their tasks professionally. Given the recent massive expansion in showroom space and the hiring proliferation, it'll be interesting to follow how well-oiled Koskela's operations become, too.

Being at the new Koskela space was a great experience for me. If the office space and environment truly do mirror and affect the culture, then I think that Sasha has a big head start on improving her business.

CHEEKY FOOD GROUP:
Cooking Up Fun

Leona Watson

Cheeky Food Group

Offers fun cooking events for corporate team building, 10 full-time employees, 20 rotating chefs, founded in 2001

Leona Watson's first job was as an administrative assistant making $13,000 a year in a remote Queensland mining town. She's a self-admittedly poor assistant who wasn't that great at filing and typing. Rather than letting her job description define her duties rigidly, she took a "no boundaries" approach and was soon doing PR and interviews on behalf of the company. And she was only sixteen at the time.

About a dozen years later, Leona Watson landed a plum gig working at Microsoft in the UK, launching Windows NT. On a whim, she took a vacation working on the crew of a tall ship, and had the 4:00 pm to 8:00 pm and 4:00 am to 8:00 am watch. While surveying the scene for submarines and other boats in the tranquility of dawn at open sea, Leona had a moment of clarity. She realized that she was in the wrong job.

Even though she had a fabulous role flying around the world and making good money in a great corporation, the big corporate thing was not her bag.

She promptly resigned her Microsoft position at age twenty-eight to move back to Australia. She'd fallen in love with a sailor on the tall ship and ended up working on a yacht with him—but earning only $1 an hour. Her friends and family were shocked at her decision to leave Microsoft, but she contended that if things didn't work out, she could always go back. In addition, how could anyone argue with working on the water beneath a smiling sun in a bathing suit and sarong?

Leona's responsibility on the boat was preparing meals. She loved the people interaction aspect. So, when she moved back to Sydney, she studied at Le Cordon Bleu to sharpen her culinary skills.

Around that time in 2001, Leona was approached by two other chefs to start a foodcompany with an innovative concept—team-building through cooking—and she took the plunge and started the Cheeky Food Group. Eventually, she bought out the other partners and has been the sole director for the last five years. Their vision was to take the joy, fun, laughter, and interaction of cooking and put it together with relationship-building at corporate events, cooking classes, and tours.

Cheeky doesn't embrace the idea of classic teacher-student relationship. Instead, they want everyone to roll up their sleeves and jump in, all while savoring great wine and grooving to fun tunes. This way, a CEO can be working alongside an assistant, and office politics go out the window. And, after 50,000 happy participants, the tally has been:

Ambulances = 0

Stitches = 0

Bandages = a handful

Today, Cheeky Food Group employs ten full-time staff and maintains a bench of twenty part-time chefs. Leona Watson claims that the company's main strategic assets are the brand, reputation, and people. She fervently believes that the brand has to be embodied by everyone, from the person answering the phone to the chefs. Even if a prospect doesn't end up buying, they should have such a strong connection to the brand that they would recommend Cheeky anyway. Cheeky actually maintains a 100 percent track record of "Yes, I'd recommend you" from their clients, which feeds into their strong reputation.

The people who embody the brand and make the reputation start to build bonds with people in their very first conversation, so that by the time of the event, clients are hugging the Cheeky staff because they have already started a great relationship. Sixty to seventy percent of Cheeky's business is repeat and referral events. So, as Leona states, "unless we really screw up, we can keep this up with no marketing." Such a great repeat customer rate is definitely a huge asset.

After ten years, Leona Watson has seen her share of triumphs and learnings as she's grown Cheeky Food Group.

Leona reveals the following insights and lessons for other entrepreneurs.

Cook up a Catchy Name

Leona came up with about ten possible names for the company. She emailed those options to fifty people for feedback. Cheeky Food Group was the second most popular name, and it didn't polarize anyone. The most popular choice was "Mad about Food": most people loved it, but some did hate it. So, in the end, Leona decided on the second-most-popular name—one that didn't rub anyone the wrong way.

Don't Be Afraid to Jump

Leona Watson astonished friends by walking away from a golden role at Microsoft, yet she said that the decision was quite easy. Leona relates that some people operate from a position of fear, but she refuses to. She even notes that, if everything went downhill with Cheeky Food Group, she would still land on her feet—she could work at a coffee shop and be okay. Leona is someone I deem a "cat." Regardless of how high the fall or how great the turbulence, she has enough skill and tenacity to land on her feet.

> *I grinned when Leona shared this anecdote with me over beers at the local taco shop where I interviewed her. It wasn't the alcohol (or maybe it was a little bit) but the fact that it's okay to jump! Along the same lines, I like to ask myself when confronted with a major decision, "what's the worst thing that will happen?" If you're like most people, you'll find a way to land on your feet. Jump!*
> —David Niu

Find the Right Ingredient for your Culture

Leona Watson states that every time that she made a wrong hiring decision, it was because she misjudged the applicant's people skills. She cautions fellow entrepreneurs to test for this, especially in a small-team environment. In addition, when pressed to choose between someone with a high culture fit but low skill level, and someone with a low culture fit but high skill level, she said that it depends on the role and how easily she can coach the weak areas. So there's no one-size-fits-all answer to that question, but she suggests always thinking about a person's own strengths and weakness, plus the company's values, before putting someone into the mix.

Listen to Your Job Applicants—On Voicemail!

Cheeky desires outgoing, energetic personalities to come on board, so to screen for those, they ask job applicants to call a specific number—and never email a résumé. The voicemail asks for basic information, such as what role you're applying for, why you would be good in that position, and what "Cheeky" X factor you would bring. Leona says that by hearing the candidate's voice and energy (or lack thereof) in the voicemail, she saves a tremendous amount of time. She can ascertain if she wants to meet the applicant within thirty to sixty seconds of hearing the voicemail.

Stick With a Review Process That Works

Cheeky Food Group's performance review contains fifteen to twenty questions and asks employees to rate themselves on a scale of 1 to 10. Some of these questions include:

- How happy are you here?
- How much do you fit into our "Own it, do it, smash it" culture?
- How effectively are you working with other people?

Leona is also a big fan of Verne Harnish and his "start, stop, continue" templates. She likes to ask her staff to come up with three bullets in each category to share. This quickly bubbles up areas for improvement and problem spots. She even took her entire team to a Verne Harnish event.

Follow Through to Keep Momentum

After the company had gone to the Verne Harnish event, they were very gung-ho. They had collected a lot of great action items to work on. Unfortunately, after the event lit the fire, there wasn't enough follow-through to maintain the momentum. So the ideas and goals died a slow death. Leona has vowed to improve this in the future, and to follow through on problem-solving after identifying the trouble areas. Leona now believes in achieving "less" but doing things well instead of setting Cheeky up to fail or get overextended with new ventures.

Performance-Based Compensation Compromise

Recently there was an employee who requested a raise, but Leona knew that the individual had areas that needed work. So they devised a three-month plan. If the individual improved in the four areas that they both agreed upon, then

Leona would provide her a raise along with back pay from the prior three months.

Keep the Focus on Your People

For the past year or so, Leona admits that she's taken her eye off of the people-management horizon. She was experiencing challenging personal and professional issues, and it culminated in losing six out of nine employees. She admits that it's tough to lose so many employees in a short period of time, but it can also be a refreshing new start. In fact, in some instances a big "clean out" is the best way to go, because if people's attitudes or performances can't be turned around, it's best to replace those folks with new team members.

Personality Tests for All

Everyone at Cheeky Food Group takes the DISC personality assessment. Leona knows that they have a lot of "type-A" personalities. Everyone is rather fiery, and that's part of their culture. However, for two recent hires, she's been looking for a better complement to herself and the team, with higher Influence and Compliance attributes. Leona is a big proponent of knowing her strengths and limitations as she hires the right team to surround her.

Candid Self-Evaluation

Leona just started working with PricewaterhouseCoopers. The consultants asked her what was holding the business back from growing. Leona said, "me." It's an amazingly self-aware answer, and Leona knows that she's why the business is as successful as it is. But she's also the reason why it hasn't reached the next level yet. She wants to make sure that there's another executive who can team up with her to take Cheeky Food Group to the next level.

Conclusion

At an early age, Leona Watson realized that work—and life, for that matter—didn't require boundaries. She could take the initiative, follow her heart, and devote herself to something that she could be passionate about, from PR to marketing to sailing to cooking. She asks, "What's the worst thing that could happen?" Even if that worst thing happens, she will always land on her feet, be able to get a job somewhere, and be OK.

This refreshing approach frees Leona, yet she's also introspective enough to know her own strengths and weaknesses. By initiating strong people-management processes like personality tests and outside coaching for herself, Leona has realized that she's part of Cheeky Food Group's limitations. Now it's up to her to help bring in the right people and get out of the way, so that they can smash the boundaries to success. Hopefully they'll quickly add to the 50,000 happy participants while maintaining the company's perfect zero-ambulances and zero-stitches track record.

GOFUNDRAISE:
Inspirational Innovation

Stuart Finlayson

Gofundraise

Software solutions for charities to reduce their costs, 16 employees, founded in 2007

Stuart Finlayson's parents started three nonprofits, and Stuart had noble ambitions to be a doctor, flying to countries in need. After university, however, Stuart Finlayson went down the marketing and advertising route before creating his own web businesses. While in London, he saw what was happening with Just Giving, the UK e-commerce company that processes the collection of charitable donations, and thought that he could improve on their model. So he started Gofundraise in 2007.

At the time, Stuart was running another business and wanted to find someone else to run this new venture. But things came full circle when he fell in love with the new organization. He particularly enjoyed returning to the community-centered values with which his parents raised him.

GoFundraise provides innovative software solutions to reduce the costs of fundraising, and empowers charities to raise even more money for their causes. In fact, for every $100 someone raises for a charity, typically only about $60-$70 of it goes to the group in need. The rest is eaten up by inefficiency and middleman fees. With GoFundraise, about 93 percent goes to the charity. That's a staggering increase of efficiency by up to 50 percent!

GoFundraise employs sixteen people who are passionate and motivated in their mission, and very committed to maintaining the company values and culture. Another huge strategic asset is the company's intellectual property. Stuart connects deeply with the emotional value of helping non-profits to raise money, but he also has a great track record in business. His commitment to innovating in the industry has resulted in robust technology that has helped many people and organizations. Their brand is well known in the nonprofit circles of Australia and has won many fans.

After five years at GoFundraise and more years at other startups, Stuart shared the following business insights.

Hire Someone With the Values That Matter Most

Stuart told me a favorite quote: "If you want a culture of smiley people, then hire smiley people." They vet every prospective employee against the company's culture and values. Even if the candidate possesses a strong skillset, if there isn't a culture fit, they'll pass on hiring the person. Everyone who is hired signs a values document which has been carefully crafted and reflects who Stuart is and how he wants his team to treat customers and each other.

> *I love Stuart's folksy advice during our interview. It doesn't get much simpler than hiring smiley people if you want your employees to smile. In the past, all things being equal, I would choose skill over fit. But today, there's no question that I would choose fit over skill. I know that if there's a strong cultural fit, I'm going to be more excited to come into work and interact with them, which I hope spills over to everyone else.*
>
> *Of course, the world is never so black and white. But I'm siding with the smiley.*—David Niu

Conduct Daily Performance Reviews

GoFundraise conducts daily performance reviews. Everything is centered on their values. If behavior doesn't align with the company's values, Stuart will bring it up to get the team member back on track.

Get Everyone Caught-up in Weekly Meetings

Stuart Finlayson realized that the team was getting a bit disjointed. They implemented a company-wide Friday 3:30 meeting. Team members take turns updating everyone else for one to two minutes on what they're working on and what's forthcoming next week. This has increased communication within GoFundraise, giving everyone a taste of what is happening in departments with which they don't usually have much contact.

Give Away Monthly Prizes for Embodying Culture

To further reinforce their culture, Stuart gives out a monthly prize (an iPad or something similar) to whoever best embodies their culture. This fun technique keeps their values front and center and top of mind.

Let Employees Set and Drive Goals

Moving forward, Stuart wants individuals to present their own goals for the month and quarter. These goals need to align with GoFundraise's vision. And if the entire team hits their self-set goals, Stuart wants to reward the entire team. GoFundraise is just starting this, so I'll be interested to follow up and see how it went and what they learned.

Give Recognition Instantly

Stuart emphasized that he always provides instant recognition. He encourages managers to never be afraid to give out positive feedback to individuals, especially in front of their peers.

Conclusion

It's important to get the culture and values of a company right. It cascades through every activity that the company does.

At GoFundraise, not only is Stuart weaving a great feel-good story, but he also obsesses over building up his company's culture. His nonprofit endeavor remains true to the noble values his parents raised him with. But the good intentions he puts into keeping his employees engaged and happy inspired me as much as anything else.

AUSTRALIA: LOOKING BACK DOWN UNDER

Stuart Finlayson reminded me that one of his favorite YouTube Videos is also one that I love. At a music festival at The Gorge Amphitheatre in Washington State, in the lawn section far from the stage, small groups sit in the sun enjoying the music. But one guy has stripped down to his shorts and shades and is not holding back—he dances like he'll never dance again. You can hear the band rocking out, but nobody else is up and moving except for this guy. You start thinking he's a weirdo and feel sorry for him as he continues to unabashedly dance by himself.

Until ... one other kid runs from somewhere across the lawn and joins the dancer in shaking it with abandon. They carry on like this for a couple of minutes before a group of other concert-goers runs up and makes it a little party. Then everybody wants to join the fun, and soon enough the whole hillside erupts with dancing.

It perfectly illustrates how when starting a business, one has to prepare to dance alone; others might not jump on board right away. But given enough perseverance, dedication, and passion—it can happen.

Along the same lines, my friend James Wong shared with me a quote, "When a company starts, a culture also starts. So why not be intentional in creating a great culture?" And the foundation of any culture comes back to the people the entrepreneur hires.

In fact, as an angel investor, I always bet on the people, because invariably the idea someone starts with requires a pivot (an educated change in business direction, strategy, or tactic). In my first two startups, Andy and I definitely needed to pivot before finding success. It's rare that someone nails the idea out of the gate. Hence, I bet on people.

The Power of People

I had interviewed five entrepreneurs in New Zealand and nine more in Australia. It amazed me that regardless of industry, size, or geography, so far everyone I interviewed could go on at length about leadership challenges, culture, and managing people. When I asked these leaders what they considered their most valuable strategic assets, most mentioned their people—not marketing, not their distribution channels, or their financial modeling.

This group of Australian business leaders also provided hope. Almost all of us have worked at a place with a bad culture, where work is just work. However, these interviewees highlighted that a culture is organic, fragile, and ever-changing. Even the best cultures can crumble with neglect. But they can also be saved and bloom again.

No Shortcuts to Building Up a Culture

Andrea Culligan helped quantify how much time it takes to repair or reboot a culture. As entrepreneurs, we send out an email on Friday and expect results the following Monday. But in reality, it took Andrea *six to twelve months* of concentrated effort before she saw sustainable change. This time horizon for cultural shifts was later independently corroborated by other interviewees. There are no shortcuts.

When Andrea and Rebekah replaced large chunks of their team, they injected much-needed new blood and helped rebuild their culture. However, turning over people makes no difference if the underlying culture doesn't change at the top. The new employees will simply become jaded, like their predecessors did. Change requires a combination of dedicated leadership plus energized staff.

Ultimately, upgrading a culture isn't easy, but it's certainly worthwhile if we look to Andrea and Rebekah's happiness as evidence.

Shifting Tides for the Family

On the family front, after a great stay in Sydney, we energetically moved on to hippie haven Byron Bay, and then to the world famous Gold Coast surf spot. We landed in a beautiful rental home. Sadly, the weather did not cooperate with our quest for vitamin D. The climate felt more Seattle-like in an uncharacteristically chilly late summer down under.

Alice and I were determined to make the most of our time there. So one early morning, we took a romantic little beach kayak excursion. Unfortunately, we'd booked it the night before a storm hit, and rather than retreat, we showed up. It reminded me of a scene out of *Cast Away,* when Tom Hanks madly endeavors to paddle past monster breakers with desperation and pathos. In our dual kayak, we paddled with all our might before getting crushed and thrown overboard. *Breaker 1, Nius 0.*

We regrouped, gathered our composure, and now had sized up our enemy. With renewed vigor, we paddled ahead. Boom! We ended up capsized into the surf again. *Breaker 2, Nius 0.* Now we were the last kayak to break past the surf. So with more experience and a bit of embarrassment and determination, we attacked the breaker again. FINALLY, we broke through. The Nius were on the scoreboard.

Meanwhile, Kayla's mother came to visit her. It was fun to add a new family member for a while. She also adored Keira, who enjoyed playing on a beach for the first time in her life.

Even though the weather didn't smile upon us, we left Byron Bay with great memories and drove to the Gold Coast eager to make more memories. Kayla was also excited to hit the Gold Coast because her boyfriend was flying in to visit too.

Unfortunately, things took a turn for the worse. Pneumonia took down the Niu adults. What started out as colds worsened with time. First Alice got so sick that she made an appointment at the clinic. She urged me to see the doctor too, but I thought I could ride it out. But then I got so sick that I asked to piggyback on her appointment. I did not want to die in Byron Bay. It was terrible to go back and forth from sweating like a pig to bundling up in all the clothes I brought, shivering under the blankets.

After so many visits to the clinic, I grabbed a business card so I could mail a thank-you note down the road. As I walked in, the receptionist cheerily recognized me and said, "Why are you back again, David?" I was disheartened. Usually on a vacation, it's the bartender who knows me on a first-name basis, not a doctor's receptionist! Still, I'm grateful we received good care and got nursed back onto our feet.

I will never again take my health nor my family's health for granted. One premise of the careercation was to travel before my health starts its inevitable decline. I'm grateful that Alice embraces taking long breaks like this throughout our lives. It definitely resonates with my decision to live more intentionally, create our own opportunities, and seize the day.

I was also amazed that little Keira came through unscathed. We were so concerned that she would fall ill. But once again, she proved her resilience. I'm glad she had ample opportunity to roam around the beach with Kayla and her mom when I was still incapacitated.

I stayed bedridden for days except to see the doctor and use the restroom. As I finally started regaining my health, I flashed back through my interviews. The stories about passion and perseverance inspired me. I also thought about how almost everyone mentioned people and culture as crucial to their business success. I couldn't wait to dive into my interviews with my first group of Asian entrepreneurs and explore this with them.

③

Korea

To gain entry to Australia, we had needed to pre-purchase exit tickets out of the country as condition of entrance. So back in New Zealand, we needed to pick which country we would visit after Australia. I lobbied for Japan. After all, we had friends in Tokyo, we love the food, and Alice speaks Japanese. Alice agreed with the advantages, but the recent tsunami, nuclear disaster, and the uncertainty around the safety of the food caused her to cross Japan off as an option.

I then tossed Korea into the ring, since I love their cuisine too. Alice pointed out that thus far, we'd been to two English-speaking countries, and we don't speak Korean. Plus, we didn't have any friends or family there. All her points were spot on, which caused me to feel uneasy and prompted me to declare that we should cross off Korea too. After a pause,

Alice stated, "Well, that's exactly the reason why we should go to Korea: because we are both nervous, and we don't know anyone there."

I smiled and began scouring the Internet for the least painful Gold Coast to Seoul flight option. Alice was right: we can't grow unless we're stretching ourselves and a little anxious. Korea it was!

The trip from the Aussie Gold Coast to Seoul became a forty-hour Amazing Race ultra-marathon endurance test. It included a cancelled flight, scrambling for a new itinerary, three layovers, and a two-hour takeoff delay. Fortunately, our little Keira's innocent good nature and our trusty au pair Kayla's great attitude helped ease the pain. Other passengers were so bored that they entertained themselves by playing with our baby.

Finally, we arrived in Seoul. After such a long journey, our bar was quite low, and we were just happy that we made it. But immediately, we were blown away. The airport was so clean and modern. Alice was impressed with all the automation and conveniences in the restroom, which helped her feel reassured right away. Little things like finding fresh and healthy food at the Korean version of 7-11, enabling us to quickly feed Keira after almost two full days of air travel, put us all at ease.

We booked an apartment through AirBnB for about a month. It was small but located in a hip, bustling neighborhood with lots of cool shops, cute little restaurants, and trendy cafes. After New Zealand and Australia, Seoul definitely created a big-city vibe with its high urban density.

East Versus West

Setting up interviews in Seoul was considerably more challenging than any other city during my careercation, maybe because many business leaders were intimidated by the notion of me "interviewing" them in English when English wasn't their first language.

Despite that, I was still extremely excited to meet the two entrepreneurs who graciously agreed to talk to me. As an Asian myself, and having studied Asian political economics as an undergraduate, I wanted to find out how Confucianism influences management practices. I was also curious about their point of view when it comes to leadership, culture, and managing people. Furthermore, I wondered how the Korean *Chaebols* (family-run conglomerates like Hyundai and Samsung) impact the business and entrepreneur community.

Finally, with only two interviews over the next month, I was looking forward to spending some quality time exploring our neighborhood and Seoul with my family. Plus I was excited to have some extended downtime to pour over my previous interviews that I had put on pause to nurse my pneumonia.

INCRUIT:
Astronomical Passion for His Work

Kwangsug Lee

Incruit

Internet recruiting, 150
employees, founded in 1998

Kwangsug Lee disarmed and instantly engaged me with a friendly, boyish charm. He shared with me that in Korea, failure for an entrepreneur is frowned upon strongly and can very negatively affect future credit and employment prospects. However, there are new government policies that are trying to address this and to spur more innovation and startups.

As a boy, Kwangsug aspired to become an astronomer and not to work at the family business despite being the oldest son. Lee's boyhood idol was none other than the famous cosmologist Stephen Hawking. After enrolling into one of Seoul's prestigious university astronomy programs to study outer space, Kwangsug also began dabbling in the online space. In 1997, he started his first online venture, Zip.org, which was a Korean directory much like Yahoo. He was very passionate about this project and felt like he was giving back to society. Kwangsug managed to harness a team of twenty to thirty part-time volunteers from his university to help him maintain and update the thousands of links on Zip.org.

Then, in 1997, the Asian financial crisis created widespread economic turmoil throughout Asia, including in Korea. Samsung resorted to firing employees for the first time in the company's history. Kwangsug began to discuss with his friend (now wife) how they could help people who became unemployed by the crisis.

Fired up after their conversation, he immediately brainstormed ideas. Three months later, in June 1998, they launched HumanLink, the first Korean Internet recruitment system that matched candidates with companies.

They ended up changing the name to Incruit, which is short for "internet recruiting." Lee wanted the brand name used as a verb, too, like "Google it" or "FedEx it." Job seekers would answer a battery of about a hundred questions and would then receive a text message if their profile matched the company's needs. This service became a godsend for the unemployed who were frantically searching for jobs during and after the crisis.

Still enrolled in school, Kwangsug was at a crossroads between the successful launch of Incruit and his university studies. Kwangsug sought advice from his father, an entrepreneur, who recommended that Kwangsug follow his passion—adding that he could always return to school later. So in 1998, Kwangsug dropped out of his prestigious astrology program to focus on Incruit exclusively.

Today, Incruit employs 150 people and is one of the leading online-recruiting sites in Korea. By building Incruit over the last fourteen years, Lee learned a lot about being a CEO and leader. He shared the following advice.

Be Resourceful

When Zip.org grew to over twenty volunteers, Kwangsug needed a more formal place for his volunteers to work, but being a student without much cash, he didn't have many options. So he approached an Internet café that was opening near his campus, cold-calling the owner. They struck a deal. Kwangsug would help the café owner with IT-related tasks in exchange for space to work.

Even more impressive: when he needed a bigger office, Kwangsug approached the Korea Association for Information and Telecommunications Promotion. He pleaded his case that the association should assist his endeavors because he was a student working on a project that would benefit the public. They agreed and lent him an office, ten desks, and a conference table, along with a fast Internet connection. He camped in that office for two years.

Not every student or young entrepreneur would have the courage to approach an Internet café owner, let alone the Korean Association for Information and Telecommunications Promotion, but working on projects that benefited the public emboldened Kwangsug. This passion translated into resourcefulness and the ability to convince others to support his cause. Every entrepreneur needs some sales skill, because at the end of the day, we're always selling to potential customers, employees, or investors.

Hire HR Position Earlier

Lee hired his first HR person when Incruit ballooned to a hundred employees. If he had to do it again, he would have set up his HR team at around forty to fifty employees instead of waiting. He believes that HR is vital in creating a company's culture, vision, mission, and processes. It's much easier and effective to start doing this sooner rather than later in a company's lifecycle.

Baking in Cultural Fit in Interview Process

Incruit's three core values are honesty, innovation, and customer-centricity. Their HR actually evaluates all potential new hires along these three parameters in order to see how they would fit into the company culture. It's very important to the company that employees embrace those values, and they balance cultural fit with skills fit. Incruit doesn't just pay lip service to the company's culture. Instead, they expose the culture and cultural expectations to employees starting in the interview process.

> *I'll definitely bake cultural fit into future interviews, starting with the job posting. I'll ask candidates if they resonate with our values, incorporated into the job description. If they do, I'll ask how they embodied those principles in past roles. Might as well be upfront and transparent to candidates, so they can decide if they want to contribute to the organization's standards.*—David Niu

Leverage Technology to Communicate with Staff

Even though Incruit leverages Microsoft SharePoint and Microsoft Messenger, Kwangsug implemented Yammer. He believes this tool further encourages communication, sharing, and innovation.

Connect with a Big Group in a Monthly Company Speech

Once a month, Kwangsug gives a state-of-the-union type speech to the company. At 150 employees, Kwangsug no longer gets the opportunity to interact with each employee, so the speech both personalizes him to employees and provides company updates. It's also a venue to reinforce company culture, vision, and mission.

The Way to a Worker's Heart is Through His Stomach

When I visited Incruit in April, they were constructing their own café on their floor. This is something that Jeremy Irish of Geocaching has done successfully in Seattle, and something I loved about Kasala in New Zealand. It's a great example of using physical space to foster and enhance company collaboration and culture.

Find What Drives You

Kwangsug Lee made up his mind at an early age that he was going to study astronomy and forgo working at his father's manufacturing company, even though he was the oldest son. Then at school, Lee realized that he loved working on public-good projects. This drove him when he worked on Zip.org and then Incruit.

Every entrepreneur needs to find something they're passionate about since to be successful, they'll be working on it 110 percent of the time and dreaming about it when they're not "working." Life is too short to work on projects for which you don't feel passion.

Conclusion

Kwangsug Lee comes across as very soft-spoken and exuded so much thoughtful charisma. So I was impressed with how he dropped out of school and also boldly cold-called the Internet café owner and the Korean association to negotiate for free space. I was most impressed by how genuine and passionate he is about his projects. He emanates a sincerity that makes Incruit's first core value of honesty feel genuine.

Rarely does a student find success right away on their first entrepreneurial venture. But passion guided Lee to help others and to build a great, sustainable organization that continues to help people find employment. Kwangsug Lee's tips reinforce the need to find what one is passionate about before—and while—embarking on an entrepreneurial journey.

ASIA EVOLUTION:
Evolving Management Styles from Midwest to Far East

John Park

Asia Evolution

Financial services for mid-tier Korean companies, 12 employees, founded in 2000

John Park's first job was at Mead Data Central in Dayton, Ohio, which is about as Midwest as it gets in the U.S. Having lived in Korea during his formative years, then in Japan for junior high and Australia for high school, John quickly noticed the differences in business culture between Korea and the U.S. He observed that the American work environment is much more open, flexible, and dynamic than the Korean work environment. This first impression would stay with him as he worked at other American blue-chip companies like McKinsey and Goldman Sachs.

While working at Goldman Sachs in New York and Seoul, John Park saw an entire middle tier of Korean companies that needed advisory work but couldn't access guidance from

Goldman Sachs because top-tier advisory companies preferred to focus only on top-tier companies. John wanted to support and make a more significant contribution to Korean businesses. So he started Asia Evolution on the auspicious first day of the millennium, January 1, 2000.

Asia Evolution, which today employs twelve people, fulfills John's vision: providing comprehensive financial consulting and growth strategies to medium-sized Korean business.

He has learned many valuable lessons over the years, putting a lot of work into the culture and helping the team develop good habits. John balances his admiration for open and dynamic styles of management by reminding himself that he works in the ever-conservative financial industry.

Today, the vision and principles of Asia Evolution are customer-centric and results-oriented while still being very attuned to the people within the company, their communication, and their teamwork. The company embraces a blend of East and West management styles that John has picked up throughout his life.

He shared the following unique insights and tips.

Implement a Sunset Policy

After John had explained this policy to me, it was quite easy to understand. People must complete whatever they have committed to doing that day before the sun sets. If they aren't done by sunset, then they must stay late to wrap it up before going home (or get approval from clients/colleagues for an alternate date of completion). They also have the flexibility to go home when projects are complete, without the pressure of unproductive "face time."

Cultural Changes Take Time

John wanted to improve certain elements of Asia Evolution's culture. Similar to any entrepreneur, he was impatient and expected more immediate results. What he learned through implementing cultural changes is that it takes time and patience. It's taken at least six months to see substantial cultural change take hold.

It's fascinating that I've never seen in popular literature how much time it takes to change a culture. As we all know, culture is organic and can improve or flounder over time. However, I never received a data point qualifying that it could take about six months for substantive changes to appear.

As an entrepreneur, I'll usually fire off an email on Friday and expect changes on Monday because I'm so impatient. But now I know I have to be patient and consistent in my investment. What I put in is what I'll get out of my commitment to creating and maintaining an outstanding culture. There are no shortcuts.—David Niu

---

Balance Your Approach to Cultural Changes

John Park learned that he needed to implement cultural changes on top of a stable platform. Otherwise, wholesale changes were too disorientating for his team to accept and embrace. So now, he eschews large changes and instead implements piecemeal changes.

Invest in Company Offsites

Two to three years ago, Asia Evolution started holding team offsites. The first year, the event was all leisure, but then John created agendas for subsequent company retreats. Now they have three offsites per year:

- Entire company offsite—They talk about where the company is heading and the big picture. They also leverage this time to create marketing materials together and to discuss any outstanding company issues.
- Project team offsite—The Project Team is the "revenue generation" half of Asia Evolution. During their time together, they review what they've accomplished thus far and what they'll need to accomplish moving forward as a team. They also receive training.
- General affairs offsite—This is the other half of the Asia Evolution team. This team focuses on internal controls and administration, and discusses goals and accomplishments as the Project Team does.

At first, John Park thought he was too busy to hold these offsites, but then he realized that he really needed them. He now views them as a successful investment in his people and business. In fact, these retreats have helped bring the team closer together, and a hundred percent of his employees provide enthusiastic, positive feedback in these meetings.

Monday 1-on-1 Dinners

When possible, John's assistant schedules dinner for him and a different team member every Monday. Since there are twelve employees, John has a private dinner with each employee about once a quarter. It is a casual, informal way for John to receive feedback on the company and even his performance. By the end of each dinner he asks, "What one thing would you do to improve Asia Evolution?" This question has been remarkably effective in eliciting thoughtful comments and suggestions—many of which John has implemented, like Friday team meetings and increased training.

Review Performance Semi-Annually

Asia Evolution divides reviews into two parts. In June at their company offsite, they provide informal 360-feedback to everyone. This review has no bearing on compensation and is meant to be more casual. They follow up with their formal 360-performance review, which does impact compensation, in December. Each employee reviews every colleague with whom they've worked to provide a 360-degree perspective. John believes this is a good rhythm of informal and then formal feedback that has worked well for Asia Evolution.

Focus Performance Reviews on Top Three Points

John's a big believer that less is more. He thinks that if an employee receives too much feedback, they can't properly process and prioritize how to improve. So he forces everyone to provide only up to three feedback points for each person.

To ensure this, the review form has only three fields—no more can be added.

Leverage Emails to Track Employee Feedback

John realizes that employees are more receptive to feedback if there are concrete examples attached. Therefore, when he emails an employee feedback or suggestions, he'll copy himself on the email. He's created a folder for each employee and organizes the copied emails into each employee's folder. During review time, he has quick and easy access to specific examples for his feedback.

Success = Passion + Perseverance

John firmly believes that success grows from a combination of passion and perseverance. Passion is necessary to keep morale and motivation high. However, entrepreneurs sometimes don't get the business model right the first time. Then they need perseverance in the face of daunting odds to keep plugging away.

Conclusion

John Park's successful career has straddled both Eastern and Western companies and philosophies. Not surprisingly, at Asia Evolution, John has adapted the best practices of both into Asia Evolution's culture and people-management processes.

For example, he's maintained a more structured work environment than what Koreans are accustomed to, but he blended it with more Western initiatives to promote collaboration, innovation, and employee buy-in.

John Park constantly seeks to learn and refine his company's culture. I believe that it's precisely this flexible approach that has enabled him to build such a successful company, one that leaders can learn from, regardless of where their companies are based.

CLOSING A CHAPTER WITH AN OPEN MIND

After my two interviews and some other interactions with folks in Seoul, both local and foreign, I had to tip my hat to the entrepreneurs in this dynamic city.

Anyone who starts a business takes on financial, emotional, and professional risks. But in Korea, these risks are magnified, especially since "success" usually means working for one of the large and safe Korean conglomerates. Someone who jumps and fails at a startup essentially destroys their personal credit and dims future career opportunities.

People who prefer to march to their own drumbeat and don't start their own business have limited options when working at a *Chaebol* (large Korean corporation). I experienced an example of how constrictive the culture could be. A friend from one of these sprawling conglomerates wanted to meet for drinks after work. I suggested 5:00 pm. He said there was no way he could make it out that early. He can't hang it up before his boss leaves, which is usually not until 7:00 pm. So we settled on 8:00 pm just to be safe.

But John and Kwansug travel a totally different course. They both managed to take the plunge, despite the risks, and created meaningful businesses. They have blended many

Western business practices into their workplace and definitely break the mold of traditional Korean corporate culture. I was so impressed with their tips, I actually adopted practices from both of them into my current business.

Lightbulb Moment

With a light networking schedule in Korea, I had time to step back and reflect on my interviews so far. I had already interviewed over fifteen entrepreneurs and collected over one hundred lessons. I made many mental notes and vowed to implement some of these inspiring and common-sense tips into my next company.

I then started looking for patterns and themes from the interviews. Regardless of geography, everyone was passionate about building a great team and company culture. But it was clearly not easy, since many of the tips the interviewees shared were lessons learned the hard way. I had previously struggled with and lost sleep over those subjects too, which I'm sure contributed to my burnout.

I started putting two and two together. My interviews highlighted that many entrepreneurs wrestle with people management and company culture even when their businesses are doing well financially. This resonated with my own experience. I reviewed my notes again and realized that almost everyone conducted annual surveys to understand their employee morale and engagement, just like Andy and I did at our companies.

Their organizations missed the same thing mind did. People and the businesses change so much and so often during the year, how could anyone get an accurate read with an annual survey? There had to be a better way. This became my lightbulb moment!

"If you can't measure it, you cannot improve it."
—Lord Kelvin

For leaders like me, there had to be a better way to get a pulse on how happy or burnt out people are before an unexpected two-weeks' notice happens, or before issues become cancerous and affect co-workers or customers. Once a year is simply too infrequent a time interval to effectively audit culture. And if people and culture are a company's top strategic assets, shouldn't we monitor them often and improve them consistently? I don't think I remember one interview when someone mentioned their accounting or finance as a top strategic advantage. Yet I'm pretty sure they monitor and review their financials constantly.

This realization catapulted me into a frenzy of brainstorming and excitement. My favorite part of being an entrepreneur is seeing people grow to their full potential. My passion for people management combined with a desire to help others with the same challenge, like the entrepreneurs I interviewed, held interesting possibilities.

I hadn't felt that energized in a while. I had fun thinking through potential solutions. It seemed that my careercation was beginning to illuminate a possible next direction for me.

Embrace the Anxiety, Keep an Open Mind

In spite of a language barrier and no friends or family, we had an amazing time in Seoul. The food in the Korean capital is affordable, diverse, and delicious. Eating out was cheaper than cooking, so we sampled different restaurants every day. Not knowing the language became more of an opportunity than a hindrance. After a bit of miming and made-up sign language, we had great meals with friendly service.

In almost no time, we felt welcomed and even part of the neighborhood, greeted by the corner shop people and the business owners that swept their tidy storefronts every morning. We also found a spacious and colorful coffee shop that had a little play area inside that became Keira's personal playground. It was one of the only places we could let Keira could run around, so we became regulars.

One thing that we didn't expect was the lack of green space for Keira to run around. The tight sidewalks were also not super-conducive to wandering around with a toddler. In hindsight, I'm sure it shouldn't have been a surprise that extremely dense cities in Asia lack an abundance of common parks and natural open space. But coming from Seattle to New Zealand to Australia, we had taken easy access to parks, trees, and water for granted.

On the flip side, because the city didn't seem that well-suited for babies, Keira was quite the novelty. Especially on the subway when Kayla, a Caucasian, had Keira strapped into the baby carrier. The Koreans, especially the older generation, loved playing with her. Even the younger folks were enthralled with her. When we went to visit the Royal Palace, Keira was surrounded by a group of schoolgirls and treated like a K-Pop star.

Kayla was very happy in Seoul because on her time off from watching Keira she could easily get around using its awesome and affordable subway system. She also met up with a friend to tour the city and was becoming as adaptable as Keira. Kayla had an open mind and enjoyed trying spicy, red chili-drenched dishes with us.

Alice also loved Seoul. It was a shopper's paradise for her. It's one of the few times I've seen her overwhelmed by too many great stores. Plus she loved the food, cleanliness, and convenience. We also had ample time to roam around as a couple since I only had two interviews.

In fact, the question we get asked the most about our careercation is, "What was your favorite place?" We always answer in unison, "Seoul!" And to think we almost missed out on this great experience. Alice was right when she insisted we come even though I had been anxious and leaning towards writing off Korea.

I Can't Feel My Face!

Not everything went smoothly. After arriving in Seoul, I was happy to see my Australian illness in the rearview mirror and grateful for a clean bill of health.

Then one day after I woke up, I complained to Alice about a dull pain behind my left ear. She suggested it was because I didn't sleep well on the new pillow. I thought, *OK, that makes sense.*

The next day, I complained that my left eye looked droopy. Alice said it's probably because the chlorine level of the pool was different in Seoul (I had taken Keira swimming the previous day). I thought, *OK, that makes sense.*

The following morning, I woke up and after brushing my teeth, began gargling water. Except I could not close my mouth and water was spewing out of it. I looked in the mirror, and it seemed like a reflection in one of those funny carnival mirrors that distort the image. Half of my face looked like the Joker in *Batman.*

I immediately ran to Alice and tried smiling. For some reason, she must've thought I was joking and burst out laughing at me! I found no humor in it at all and still give her a hard time about it to this day.

It was really a scary moment. We were in a foreign country where we couldn't speak the language, didn't know where to go for health care, and half of my face was paralyzed like I was ready for Halloween.

Alice immediately called our brother-in-law, who is an emergency room doctor in L.A., to see if he could provide guidance. He had known about my health scare in Australia, and after a battery of questions, he was pretty sure I was suffering from Bell's Palsy. Of course, the word "palsy" didn't exactly calm me down, but he told us the questions we needed to ask a doctor in Seoul to confirm the diagnosis. He also reassured us that in most cases, the paralysis subsides naturally over time.

After searching online, we rushed to Seoul National University Hospital. I was immediately hooked up to electrodes as they shocked different areas of my face to determine my level of paralysis (yes, getting shocked on the eyelid was the worst). They confirmed that I did have Bell's Palsy, which may have been an opportune infection after my immune system was weakened by my illness in Australia.

A bright spot to this latest health setback was my amazing experience being medically treated in Seoul. The facilities and equipment all looked new, and the staff was professional. They even provided me with a translator. I received medication and orders to just wait it out. All in all, my visit only cost about $50! That was also a pleasant surprise.

I learned to drink water (and Korean beer) by tilting my head to one side. I also took my medication on time and tried to get as much rest as possible. Once again, I realized that I could not take health for granted. I felt even more grateful that we took the careercation and blazed those memories while we did. It's easier to bounce back now than it will be down the road, I think.

It did make me wonder, though—had I taken better care of my sickness in Australia, rested more, or treated the pneumonia sooner, might it not have gotten so bad? I know most issues get better when tackled head on—problems at home, with health, and in business. Sure, time heals wounds. But could I have avoided this latest illness if I was more diligent sooner? Of course, this health scare would also play into the planning of our next stops on our careercation.

Finally, I did slow down which afforded me the time to review my past interviews and see the pattern that led to my lightbulb moment. So I chose to think positively, that what happened in Seoul was a blessing in disguise. And it still is our favorite destination during our journey.

④

China

The next stop was Shanghai. Shanghai has held a special place in my heart since I first visited in 1995, when I was on winter break from Peking University. I loved my first exposure to Shanghai. My mother's side of the family is from the Shanghai-Ningbo area, so the language was familiar to me, and the food was like home cooking.

When I was studying in China twenty years ago, I met one of my best friends, Jeff Hu, literally on the Great Wall. Jeff was also studying abroad at Peking University. Not only did Jeff and I study abroad together, we were the best man at each other's weddings, Jeff worked with me on my first business, and he has twin girls that are only a couple months younger than Keira.

For three months, Keira's main interaction had been with adults, so it delighted me to see her play with Jeff's kids. Plus, I know Jeff's lovely wife, Lina, whom he met and married in Shanghai. As a bonus, we stayed with them during our time there.

Jeff's *ayi* helped with childcare and cooking. *Ayi* means "auntie" in Chinese, and most families call their hired caretakers by this term of endearment. Jeff and Lina lived in a nice gated high-rise with a children's center and pool. We definitely felt we could get used to this level of comfort.

I also set up a good round of interviews and looked forward to further corroborating the pain points around managing people and creating culture that the other interviewees revealed to me. In addition to Jeff, I interviewed a handful of other ex-pats forging their way in the Chinese marketplace: a South African fruit importer, an Aussie restaurateur, and a Taiwanese video game chief. After my interviews in Korea, I also wanted to see how socially acceptable it is to start a business in China, even if it fails.

I got to run my fledgling business concept by Jeff. I highly respect his opinion because he worked at Aon Hewitt, which does a lot of HR consulting. Plus he runs his own staffing and recruiting firm. I was curious if my possible solution would also help him run his business more efficiently. I interviewed him and learned some great people management and HR ideas. I knew he wouldn't sugarcoat his thoughts and wouldn't be afraid to throw water on my idea.

ATOMIC RECRUITMENT:
What Have I Done For You Lately?

Jeff Hu

Atomic Recruitment

Recruiting agency for multinational companies in China, 45 employees, founded in 2005

Jeff Hu learned two key lessons growing up in Southern California. First, his parents raised Jeff to respect, care for, and listen to others. Today, he embodies this lesson when he "leads by sharing."

Second, in his first job at The Gap in high school, he found that no job was ever going to be easy. That's why they call it "work." So at an early age, he realized the importance of career planning before entering the workforce after college.

True to form, fresh out of university he became a management consultant, worked in startups, and started his own venture in China. At the same time, his wife Lina Li and a business partner started Atomic Recruitment in Shanghai in 2005. In 2008, Jeff sold his company, completed his MBA, and joined Atomic.

Atomic, a recruitment agency that places mid- to senior-level Chinese talent into multinational companies in China, employs forty-five people and has offices in Shanghai and Beijing. Since coming onboard, Jeff has taken over the business development, marketing, and HR operations from his wife (who has since switched careers), doubled the number of clients, and instituted a level of professionalism that distinguishes Atomic from competitors.

Because Atomic's clients are foreign multinational corporations, they expect and demand a very high level of service. Jeff and his partners know how to meet and exceed the expectations that many domestic operations can't match. Atomic that also separates themselves from the pack by their use of technology. Even back when they had fifteen or so employees, the firm invested in their future by building up their technical infrastructure to a level that you might find at a 100-person recruiting company. Consequently, Atomic's CRM and databases are very robust and flexible enough to scale their support to even a hundred more personnel.

Another advantage that Atomic Recruitment has over other firms is a culture that fosters a family-like environment, one in which employees feel comfortable enough to stay instead of looking for other opportunities in a market that is replete with options. To Jeff, running Atomic like a family business means maintaining strong ethics and creating trust with the staff through fairness, transparency, and inclusion.

Jeff and the team spent a lot of time creating the aforementioned competitive advantages. Of course, he's experienced his share of both wins and setbacks throughout this process. As Jeff reflected on Atomic's growth and success, he revealed the following guidance and learning:

Celebrating Performance

At Atomic, a big board lists and stack-ranks everyone's name and sales numbers. So there is no hiding and no hidden agendas. On the other side of the coin, every quarter starts with a kickoff that honors high achievers, top billers, and staff who hit their targets. They give away five to ten awards during this celebration. They have even taken a company trip to Hainan Island, China's tropical beach resort, after hitting a company stretch goal.

Many businesses have goals for their staff and rigidly stick with them despite changes in macroeconomic conditions. At Atomic, Jeff adjusts employees' quarterly bonuses every quarter depending on the economy and how a person is performing. Since 80 percent of employee compensation is commissions, these additional bonus-based goals are variable in order to keep employees motivated and challenged without being daunting.

Buddy System for New Hires

To get people integrated and acclimated to Atomic's culture, each new hire is assigned a buddy who introduces the new hire to everyone else. This buddy is also the new hire's go-to person for questions about the company's operations and policies. They don't discriminate based on role: the buddy system applies for interns as well as management consultants.

Clear Career Development Path

Jeff Hu realizes that offering a transparent career path is one key to keeping talented staff members. This includes mentoring as well as taking a personal interest in their career goals (such as providing support to get into a Master's program). He spends a lot of time balancing the goals of each staff member while aligning them with Atomic's goals.

Set Culture Free

Like many companies, Atomic has a mission and cultural values. And like many companies, these points are expressed in a memo and then mothballed: even the executives can't recite them. Jeff feels that Atomic's cultural values are trapped in their brochures and not fully communicated to the company.

One strategy would be to spotlight and agree upon the values. There is some push and pull between Jeff and his business partner, who has a more traditionally Chinese view that too much time spent on communication and reviews takes away from the bottom line, while Jeff is focusing on retention.

At Atomic, they have a good motto: "Placing people with energy." I think that once the vision, mission, and values are evangelized (which Jeff was on the cusp of re-initiating at the time of this interview), Atomic's culture as a competitive advantage will only strengthen.

Don't Change Company Policies to Police Minority

At one point, Atomic initiated policy changes specifically to target the actions of one or two people. Everyone in the company knew that the changes were meant to address these individuals' behaviors. Upon reflection, Jeff doesn't think it was a good business or cultural decision, and in hindsight would have addressed the situation directly with the individuals without affecting the other 95 percent of the company.

> *I wholeheartedly agree. I've been guilty of tweaking company policy to police one or a handful of abusers. It was obvious to everyone why we made the change and whom the change targeted. But unfortunately the non-abusers were being punished, too.*
>
> *Moving forward, I want to create a culture of high accountability where people hold themselves accountable to each other. If I have to discipline someone, then the conversation will probably focus on their long term fit with the culture we're trying to create and jealously protect.*—David Niu

Grow with Executive Coach

Atomic has hired an outside consultant to create a fair and comfortable environment for their executives to communicate transparently amongst themselves. In Jeff's mind, the next step is to take the process to another level by having the coach conduct a 360 review for each executive. This then creates a nonthreatening forum to discuss how the executives can improve individually and as a team. Transforming a company culture—as we know from listening to all of these executives trying to do it—takes time, and it starts with buy-in from top management. Then, mid-level managers are more committed to forward-thinking practices, and the whole company is in sync.

Conclusion

I think Jeff Hu's parents would be proud that their son took their life lessons to heart, and now "leads by sharing" at Atomic. I think that recruitment can be a very transactional, numbers-based, "what have you done for me lately?" type of business. So it pleased me to see that with Jeff's deft touch and influence, Atomic is incorporating sustainable and hard-to-copy advantages such as professionalism, transparency, and culture that endears the company to their clients and candidates. As Atomic continues to flourish, I think that the next evolution of the company will be for management to grow with their executive coach, and set their culture free.

RADIANCE:
Leveling Up to the Boss Stage

Monte Singman

Radiance Digital Entertainment

Computer game developer, 35
employees, founded in 2005

Monte Singman had his first job at age fifteen, heaving heavy loads of flyers and stuffing neighborhood mailboxes in Taiwan's stifling summer heat. He was trying to earn enough money to buy an Apple II knockoff for $300. Even though it was backbreaking work, Monte realized that he was still just a commodity to the flyer company.

Monte kept this lesson in the back of his mind as he grew up and dove into developing gaming software. He eventually wrote a fortune-telling software program that became a hit in Taiwan, and then took his skills to Silicon Valley, where he realized that instead of being a commodity, he was a highly valued talent. But with this recognition came a new challenge:

in order to grow professionally, Monte had to learn to manage people. He didn't want to make the mistake of treating his team like commodities.

Monte Singman started Radiance in 2005, and today the company employs thirty-five people in Shanghai. Monte has worked on hit titles at small and large game studios and has learned many valuable lessons on how to build a successful company. He shared the following experiences and lessons.

Open-Door Solution

Monte has long maintained an open-door policy; however, at first, employees rarely came to talk to him. He realized that waltzing into your boss's office to discuss company matters was just too foreign a concept to Chinese employees. Monte kept emphasizing and reinforcing the policy to his team, and over the years more and more employees walked through his door. But even today, they still don't do it enough, and people don't speak up in team meetings. So Monte holds weekly 1-on-1s with his direct reports. When he looks back at what he perceives to be his best period as a manager, he spent a huge part of his week on these meetings.

If You're Thinking about Firing Someone, You Will

Thirteen years ago, Monte Singman's mentor shared with him that, if Monte was thinking about firing someone, then he undoubtedly would end up letting go of that person. Monte thought that that philosophy was flawed because he believed that people can change and be mentored. In fact, he took it as somewhat of an insult, because Monte himself had undergone tremendous personal growth over the years as a result of coaching by his bosses.

It's hard to believe that Monte was once a shy, introverted programmer. He has such an engaging and commanding presence now. Nevertheless, after many years and many employees, Monte relayed that his mentor's saying has withstood the test of time and proven to be right. Investing in improving your star players is one thing, but putting in too much time to change someone who was never a good fit is a waste of time.

Don't Get Too Close to Direct Reports

Monte strives to create a collegial, friendly, and laid-back work environment. Yet in years past, he made the mistake of getting too close to some of his direct reports. Consequently, because of those friendships, he found it much more difficult to coach these team members' weaknesses. Today, Monte aims to achieve a balance of approachability without being too chummy.

When the Going Gets Tough, the Tough Get Weird

He said that he heard this phrase about two decades ago, but never knew what it meant until recently. Now, he gets it. Monte explains that if you're trying to solve a challenging problem and all the logical solutions are exhausted, then the answer requires out-of-the-box creative thinking. So, if you keep bumping against a wall when dealing with a dilemma, maybe there's a way to go over, around, or under the wall instead of repeatedly running into it.

Never Ridicule Ideas, but Do Laugh at Yourself

Related to "The Tough Get Weird," Monte's philosophy is to never dismiss others' ideas or laugh at them. He encourages and entertains all ideas because he never knows when he may need a weird solution. He believes that a work culture that ridicules or punishes people for their ideas stifles creativity. When he does hear what he initially considers a bad idea, he tempers his language so as not to discourage someone for speaking up.

To make a point about embracing differences, Monte even dressed up as Santa Claus during Christmas to hand out presents, which floored all of his Chinese team members! In China, a typical boss would fear losing face by doing such a thing. He had to catch the employees smiling because they were too scared to laugh at him and risk getting fired. This lighthearted, approachable attitude has become his signature. If you've met Monte, you know that he must have played a great Santa Claus, with his facial hair and his gentle smile.

Truth Withheld = [Pain * Interest] Compounded by Time

You don't want people to be surprised during their performance reviews. If they are not doing well, they should know before then.

This resonated with me immediately when Monte told me that he espouses a no-surprises review policy. From his experience, any time the truth is withheld or sugarcoated, it incurs "interest pain," which is pain compounded over the length of time that the truth had not been revealed.

I think that Monte would agree that this axiom could also be applied when you are thinking about firing someone but delay doing it. There's short-term, immediate pain from postponing the deed. The pain gets compounded by the toxicity that occurs when that person interacts not just with others on the team, but with suppliers, vendors, and customers, too. Be honest and fair with feedback, and eliminate surprises. This minimizes pain for all the parties involved.—David Niu

Shelve Ego and Ask for Help

Monte's presence fills up a room when you meet him, so it was refreshing to hear that he frequently asks others for help. In his experience, business owners are often too ego-bound to ask for support. With his approach, Monte gets to learn and grow continuously as an entrepreneur and leader, even though he's already had his share of success.

Conclusion

It's gratifying to see someone as accomplished as Monte Singman end an interview with this tip: it always makes sense to put the ego aside and ask for help when it's needed. I think that it's this humble philosophy that makes his open-door policy feel genuine to his team, and that enables him to keep growing and improving as a leader. By the same token, since he's not embarrassed to ask for help, he's also generous about giving help, exemplified by his sharing of lessons and tips that he learned the hard way.

ORIGIN DIRECT ASIA
A Bushel of Wisdom

Jason Bosch

Origin Direct Asia

Leading importer and trader of fruit, 9 employees, founded in 2008

I was excited to talk to Jason Bosch, a South African running a fruit import and trading operation in Shanghai called Origin Direct Asia. Jason definitely met one of my main goals in the careercation—to connect with entrepreneurs of diverse backgrounds. With Jason, I learned a bunch about the fruit business, and I would never have guessed that the only fruits valuable enough to ship via airfreight are early season cherries and mangos!

Jason started his career in a South African government outfit that inspected and certified all fruits and vegetables shipped out of the country, maintaining their country's high agricultural standards. Jason inspected fruit all over South Africa and quickly learned that he was allergic to bureaucracy. To illustrate: in 1998, the agency was conducting all inspection write-ups by hand, which then required an admin to transcribe, type, and return the report for review. Jason lobbied to use a laptop, which would result in more efficient and accurate reporting. After his request had been sent up one level after another over many weeks, his request was denied.

Another South African fruit exportation company, AfriFresh Group, offered him an opportunity to run the operations, sales, and marketing groups for the Far East and Middle East regions. Jason jumped at the chance. While in that role, Jason noticed an increasingly large appetite for fruit in Hong Kong and China. Sales were way up in East Asia while other international markets remained flat. Nobody understood the consumption habits and sales process in China, in spite of exponential growth there. South Africa did not have anybody "on the ground" to investigate, explain, or maximize the potential in Chinese fruit import markets.

In 2008, Jason Bosch planted the seed of moving an outpost to Shanghai. He got enthusiastic support from AfriFresh to run a joint venture and opened up Origin Direct. Today, Origin Direct Asia is a leading importer and fruit trader. The agency employs six people in Shanghai, two in Chile, and one in South Africa. They import fruit not just from South Africa, but from South America, the U.S., Egypt, Australia, Mexico, and smaller countries as well. Here is some guidance from Jason on grafting the business practices of East and West.

You Catch More Bugs with Honey Than with Vinegar

Jason learned that the confrontational, aggressive work style typical in South Africa and other Western countries doesn't work well in Shanghai, so he had to adapt his work approach. He started by taking a more active role in becoming a respected friend, as opposed to an aloof boss or best buddy. Because of the deferential communication styles that Chinese people typically have with their employers, in order for Jason to get creative help on problems, his employees needed to find him trustworthy and approachable. Acting distant or detached from his workers kept them following orders, but didn't result in innovation from the team.

Customer-Centric Feedback Replaces Annual Reviews

Origin Direct Asia was the first business that I had encountered on my trip that has never conducted formal employee reviews. Instead, they rely on setting goals to determine performance-based bonuses and raises.

Jason also procures another active feedback loop: after the season is over, he actively asks customers what the company can do better and what they have done well. Jason receives comments for both the company and the employees who interact with the customer. Then he aggregates and passes the feedback on to the proper parties, in order to provide customer-centric insights.

In spite of not having a formal review process in place, Jason has promoted many employees from within. In almost five years, he has only lost two employees, and one of those was due to illness. Since the younger staff members have seen the company flourish, they feel empowered to learn and grow into new roles. In fact, two very junior employees who started off in admin and filing have since become valuable assets to Origin Direct, one as head of logistics and the other as a junior accountant.

> *This tip definitely caught my attention. The nuance that struck the deepest chord with me is getting feedback from customers about how their products and team are doing. Moving forward, it would be great to leverage technology to get a pulse on how customers perceive the company's offering and how they view employee performance. Then I'd share that feedback back with the team to highlight those employees who are going above and beyond, and to identify which clients need to be triaged with extra attention before they jump ship.*—David Niu

Coaching the Coach

Another consequence of working in a culture that has to cajole communication from subordinate employees is that Jason receives little feedback on his performance as a manager. At a corporate learning event, he was bowled over by how effectively an outside coach interviewed another executive, bringing up and exploring very important issues. It inspired Jason, and he's thinking about who can help him in this regard.

Let Go and Empower to Grow

Jason used to dread holidays and vacations, fretting that things wouldn't get done when he was gone. Upon reflection, he realized that he created this situation by not enabling the team around him. Even as a student, he was acknowledged as a talented individual performer—on the rugby pitch or in school—who struggled as a leader because he didn't delegate enough. Jason connected the dots and realized that this tendency reflected a managing weakness at Origin Direct Asia. There are too few people in the company that fully know operations; consequently, there are too many potential points of failure if they lose key staff members. This jeopardy limits their growth.

For this and other reasons, Jason appreciates the Entrepreneurs' Organization. As a member, he can receive coaching around hiring senior staff. Hopefully, with a more empowered team, Jason can take a truly relaxing vacation— rather than working on his laptop while cruising on a boat during his honeymoon.

Know your Market Intimately

This is the only foreign fruit importation company with an office in China. At first, the company considered just having a South African representative. Being in-country, not just visiting from the home office, has enabled Jason to get accurate market information, to intimately know the supply chain, and to receive feedback without physical, cultural, or language barriers. On the other hand, Jason acknowledges that to a foreigner, the Chinese culture is still very complicated and challenging. In his search for a right-hand man to whom he can delegate business operations, Jason is open to bringing a local on board. Then his team can develop even deeper relations with clients and gain a better understanding of the local market.

Conclusion

I learned that the Chinese buy fruit with their eyes because many fruit purchases are meant as gifts designed to impress the recipient. Large, perfect-looking (non-organic) fruits are highly valued. I also learned that Jason Bosch's favorite fruits are seedless grapes; that pesticides are quite safe; and that it can be extremely challenging for a foreigner to thrive in another country, especially from a people-management perspective.

Jason's tips reminded me that even though management styles need to be localized, some best practices, such as customer-centric feedback and employee empowerment, remain valuable regardless of a business's culture of origin.

THE LARDER:
Rigor + Artistry = Success in the Restaurant Business

Steve Baker

The Larder

Restaurant, founded in 2012

When I met Steve Baker in Shanghai, he struck me as a gregarious, jocular, somewhat imposing figure—the type you imagine having played soccer or rugby all day long as a child. So it was amusing to hear Steve recount that, growing up in Australia, he rarely played outside. Instead he slavishly watched cooking shows, mesmerized; he took notes and proclaimed to his mother that he wanted to be a chef when he grew up. Steve didn't disappoint, pursuing his dream with vigor by winning cooking competitions and working as a celebrated chef around the world before opening his first restaurant, Mesa Manifesto, in Shanghai.

I interviewed Steve Baker as he was poised to open The Larder Bar and Grill, his second restaurant in Shanghai. I admit that I had no idea what a "larder" was, so it was refreshing when Steve discussed the concept behind his new establishment.

Steve described a larder as similar to grandma's pantry, with food, sauces, chutneys, and other staples. When people come to The Larder Bar and Grill, he wants the vibe to be similar to coming over to his house for dinner—warm, dependably tasty, and with an open kitchen.

When you have an open kitchen at home, it's easy enough to keep it tidy and sanitary, but it's much riskier for a restaurant to open their kitchen, coffee, wine, and chef's stations for show to diners. Sanitation aside, the open strategy is part of Steve's mission to demystify Western food to the Chinese audience. Cozy furnishings and a fun, interactive experience appeal both to locals who are looking for consistently good food and to expats who want a hearty, familiar meal.

Steve embraces the challenges of mixing cultures—both on the menu and in the restaurant's operations. He shared the best practices he's implemented to create not only a great restaurant but also a great business.

Mandatory Daily and Weekly Huddles

The main way that Steve Baker achieves a consistently great experience is by focusing on constant communication and training. Steve leverages the daily and weekly huddle technique that Verne Harnish espouses in *Mastering the Rockefeller Habits*. To get the ball rolling, Steve held weekly 1-on-1 mentoring sessions with his department heads to emphasize how important these regular meetings were. Initially, he encountered resistance, since his Chinese staff was not familiar with this approach, and his Western staff thought it was, quite frankly, a waste of time to hold all these meetings.

After six to nine months, Steve was able to establish a healthy daily and weekly meeting rhythm. However, it was not easy to get there, and Steve was the coach, cheerleader, and enforcer who ensured that his organization embraced these huddles. During these meetings, they discuss goals, competitions, and problems. The communication plus the mentoring not only improved the organization's performance, but also improved retention, which Steve saw as a tangible validation for his approach.

Empower Staff

Steve Baker is a strong proponent of empowering his team. For example, when the restaurant was new, his department heads would come to him in a paralyzed state, looking for approval and guidance when they needed to hire or fire. After continual training and 1-on-1s, Steve pushed these managers to make the critical decisions themselves.

Today, Steve doesn't meet any candidates until they are in the final stage of the interview process. And if a staff member doesn't work out, the buck doesn't stop with Steve. The department head is responsible for documenting and letting the person go. It would have been easy for Steve to be a control freak on this issue, yet by empowering his team, they are happier and more engaged, and Steve can then focus on big-picture issues.

Train and Promote Within

I chuckled when I heard that Steve's #2 chef drove a taxi six years ago, and that a supervisor used to wash dishes. But Steve was deadpan when recounting these promotions because he invests heavily in training, positioning it as the pathway to promotion. He puts his money where his mouth is by seeking to train, groom, and promote internally first. I think this is another reason why their retention rate is better than the industry average.

> *I'm a big fan of training and promoting from within. Usually, my first interview question is, "If we meet again in 10 years, what will you be proud to have accomplished?" Then I consider if we're the right place to get that individual to their goals as quickly as possible.*
>
> *If a new hire's goal is to start a company or go to business school, at least I know from the start and will help direct their career arc in that direction. But if they are looking to grow within the business, then I think proactively about the steps and skills needed. I always want to give insiders a first shot since they've committed to us.*—David Niu

Reward Team versus Individuals

Oftentimes, Steve's restaurant hosts internal revenue goals. Instead of just incentivizing the servers if they hit the goals, Steve involves the entire department. He posts the targets where the entire department can see their objective and how they're progressing towards it. When they succeed, everyone gets to share in the spoils of victory.

Strategically Stagger Bonuses

In China, it's common practice that employees receive a Chinese New Year bonus before returning to their hometown to celebrate in February. However, Steve Baker noticed that many employees would take the bonus and then hop to a different job after Chinese New Year. To offset this, Steve provides them a portion of their bonus prior to Chinese New Year. Then, he holds their annual performance review in March when they return, at which point they may receive the other part of their bonus plus any raise or promotion. This schedule more naturally integrates the big holiday bonus season with the review cycle.

Enjoy Market "Research"

For a restaurant guy like Steve, market research means having a solid night out with his management team. They'll visit competitors and review the service, products, menus, and decor. When he does this, he takes only a couple of people from the same department, so that they're focused on competitive observation. If he invites too many people, it devolves into a social event. So he'll go with his small team to one place for a starter, another place for a main course, and another place for dessert. It really gets the team fired up, and they leave with the attitude, "we can do better than that!" which they bring back to their coworkers.

Attitude Trumps Skills

The eternal debate: all things being equal, would you hire someone with a better attitude but poorer skills, or someone with better skills but a poorer attitude? Steve said that he almost always prefers attitude over skill since he can train needed skills. This is particularly true for entry- to mid-level roles. He looks for the right body language, service ethics, and manner. Yet he did offer me the caveat that, if the role is more senior, then skills play a bigger role in the decision.

Conclusion

It's always great to meet someone like Steve Baker who is living his childhood dream. Even more impressive is the rigor (meetings, 1-on-1s, training) that he instills into his business culture, which blends with the artistry of creating tasty dishes and drinks. I believe that it's this balanced approach that has made Steve so successful, especially as a husky Australian in Shanghai. Fittingly, as Steve loomed over me to shake my hand after the interview, he cracked a quick smile and then was already set to jump into a 1-on-1 mentoring meeting.

SHANGHAI SURPRISE

At first, we liked that we didn't have to leave Jeff's nice gated community except for my interviews. But after a while, we were getting stir-crazy after previously doing so much exploring on our careercation.

Because of the severe air pollution, we were cautioned against going outside. Plus the green space is limited only to the courtyard in the center of all the towering condominiums.

Jeff and Lina are extremely gracious hosts, and their family definitely enjoys a comfortable lifestyle. At the same time, it was interesting to see the tradeoffs people make to take advantage of the booming Chinese economy.

Everyday life in Shanghai was so different than in Seattle. We all make compromises when having a family, becoming an entrepreneur, or choosing a place to live. But Alice and I knew that despite all the allures of Shanghai, its pace, the environmental issues, and lack of nature meant Shanghai just isn't our cup of tea. Which is funny, because we originally looked forward to visiting Shanghai. Seoul had been only a runner-up because of the tsunami tragedy in Japan, but Seoul turned out to be our favorite place. It just shows that everything works out for the best.

Business on the East Coast of the East

If the family side of the Shanghai visit was a bit of a letdown, the business side was exciting and eye-opening. The vibe felt like the opposite of Korea. In China, it felt like it was only a matter of time before someone should try their hand at starting a business. Entrepreneurship is much more welcomed and encouraged in China, where I didn't detect that dark stigma that accompanied failure in Korea.

Familial piety remains a strong cultural value in China in spite of all the rapid changes. This doesn't transcend to the workplace. The proliferation of opportunities in this economic boom lures young workers to jump from job to job.

Retention is a huge problem for business owners. During Chinese New Year, the country practically shuts down as people return to their hometowns. All these entrepreneurs worry their staff won't return after the New Year. Many employees just take a new job and disappear. Consequently, the entrepreneurs all could relate to my story of the unexpected two weeks' notice out of the blue. In China, employees provide insult to injury by just taking another opportunity without giving notice.

Jeff Gives Me the Green Light

Jeff and I arranged some time to go out without the kids or wives so we could dive into my new business idea. I shared with him my struggle to understand how my team was feeling, especially my concerns about morale and retention. It felt like a universal challenge that I shared with almost all entrepreneurs I interviewed. He nodded. So far so good.

I then outlined my approach to address this pain point.

- **Frequent.** Once a year engagement surveys don't cut it. I'd check in with employees once a week to start to get their temperature. The questions would change week to week, but we'd ask one consistent question to gauge the employees' happiness over time.
- **Lightweight.** Since we're trading a big employee survey at the end of the year for much more frequent pulses, I would limit each survey to only one question. Not only is this good for response rates from the staff, but it also helps reduce the analysis paralysis that Andy and I felt when the deluge of responses came back. We often didn't know where to even start digging for insights since there were so many data points.
- **Anonymous.** Employees need a safe environment to share what's going well and where improvements are needed. I felt that anonymity had to underpin the offering, and that leaders had to focus on the "what," not the "who," to spark positive change.
- **Automated.** I know that entrepreneurs are busy and guilty of rushing to urgent issues at the expense of important matters that (seemingly) can wait. To that end, we would design the survey questions based on research, suggestions, and best practices to load into the solution. This makes it super simple for the CEO. Since the questions are consistent, we could provide benchmarks. Lacking comparison was an Achilles' heel when Andy and I did our own surveys. We never knew

if a 7.5 was good or bad since we didn't have anything to compare it to.

After taking it all in, Jeff exclaimed that if we had a system like this, he'd definitely buy it. He did push back on localization and translation support. Plus, he wasn't sure if the automated approach would resonate with entrepreneurs, who can be micromanagers.

But his enthusiasm caused me to toss and turn that night. Now I couldn't wait to get to Vietnam for another gut-check with my friend Dave Hajdu in Saigon. If he thought the idea was compelling, his company could even prototype it for me.

⑤

Vietnam/ Shenzhen

After staying about two weeks with Jeff in Shanghai, we were all excited to go to Vietnam. Unfortunately, a hand, foot, and mouth disease outbreak was killing kids in Vietnam. This scared Alice. So we decided that I would continue to Vietnam solo while they would fly to Shenzhen to spend quality time with Alice's father.

From the local four-hour plane ride from Shanghai (not counting the four-hour delay at the airport) to the end of our stay in Shenzhen, what fascinated others and intrigued us as well was how differently we seemed to raise Keira. We encouraged her to be autonomous and explore.

There were definitely eyebrows raised when we did not attend to Keira the way other families responded to their toddlers. I'm sure part of this can be attributed to China's one-child policy. It leads grownups to dote on children. There may be four grandparents putting all their lovin' into their one and only grandchild—not to mention parents and nannies catering to the same baby.

So we were interested to see how Alice's family would treat Keira, especially since this would be the first time both grandfather and grandmother had seen her.

On the work front, I didn't have any interviews scheduled for Shenzhen and only Dave Hajdu was scheduled in Saigon. David had also attended the EO Queenstown conference where I started my careercation, and I couldn't wait to get his feedback on my idea. I would get his perspective after many late nights talking about my pursuit of personal and professional happiness with a careercation jumpstart.

VINASOURCE:
Creating a Culture that Does NOT Suck

Dave Hajdu

Vinasource

Software design and development outsourcing company, 42 employees, founded in 2007

Dave Hajdu's first job was at age fourteen, mowing lawns in his hometown in the U.S. He made flyers on his Commodore 64 and dot-matrix printer, negotiated with clients, wheeled out the lawn mower, and got his friends to do the mowing! His second job was at McDonald's, and he learned right away that working for someone else "sucked." So, at an early age, Dave knew that working for himself would always be the way to go.

Many years later, Dave went to Vietnam to help a friend with a software development project. He became enamored with the opportunities that Vietnam offered, especially as a potential software outsourcing base. At the same time, Dave's good friend, Benjamin "Ahn Ahn" Liu was doing software consulting in the U.S., and one of Benjamin's clients needed to outsource some development. They decided to combine forces and started Vinasource in January 2007.

Today Vinasource employs forty-two people and is a full-service, boutique software design and development outsourcing company. Vinasource focuses on four technologies: PHP, .NET, Android, and IOS. Surprisingly, Vinasource has conducted zero sales and marketing: their client base comes strictly from referrals. Obviously, this speaks volumes about the good work they do. In addition to having great coders, Vinasource managers have solid English skills and communicate effectively both externally and internally. Dave has invested heavily in training and mentoring these managers along with the entire company.

In a company that revolves around placing people to work on client projects, Dave acknowledges how important his staff and managers are, but what really makes Vinasource hum are its human resource processes. People come and go, especially in the outsourcing business. Vietnam has a high turnover rate relative to the rest of Asia. However, during the last five years, Vinasource has improved HR practices to mitigate high turnover and continue to grow. This includes better interviewing, onboarding, training, and reviews.

As an American building Vinasource in Saigon from the ground up, Dave has experienced missteps along with successes. He shares the following experiences and guidance for other entrepreneurs around the globe who need to mitigate HR "pain" with helpful procedures.

Hire HR Person Earlier

Dave hired his first HR person when Vinasource grew to thirty-five employees. In hindsight, he would have hired someone when the company was around ten or fifteen employees because their current HR person's responsibilities include much more than a traditional HR role. For example, in Vietnam, employees are really into events such as team lunches, parties, and outings. These have a very positive effect on company culture, cohesion, and retention. The Vinasource HR person helps Dave to coordinate events in addition to the more traditional HR tasks.

Hiring earlier and implementing more of these corporate events would definitely have helped build the company culture and improved retention when Vinasource was building out its staff. Having this key personnel member has helped to improve processes so much that the quick rate of improvement in a short time has helped make up for the missteps of the past.

Integrate New Hires in a Welcoming Way

Dave realized that if a new employee worked past their one-month anniversary, they would most likely stick around. He designated the first month as the "danger zone" since many new hires were coming onboard and then quitting abruptly. He knew that he had to redesign the entire new-hire process.

Now, when a candidate interviews, each one immediately receives a packet with a Vinasource pen and folder that includes the company's vision, mission, and cultural values. If Vinasource makes an offer to a candidate, now someone from the company will always schedule an in-person meeting over coffee to review the offer. Previously, they may have done this over Skype or email.

On an employee's first day, Vinasource has a very specific agenda. The HR staff ensure that the new employee meets with every member of the team they will be working with and that the team goes out to lunch together. The new hire reviews the company's vision and culture and then dives into the software tools used by Vinasource. They also receive a company T-shirt. By redesigning the new-hire integration process, onboarding is smoother and retention has dramatically increased.

> *I can learn from Dave in this area. I've been guilty of investing so much time to find and hire the right candidate. But when they would start, I didn't invest nearly enough time to make their first days and weeks memorable. Moving forward, I'm not going to overlook this vital first impression because I think this has been a weak link for me.*—David Niu

Leverage Surveys

Vinasource conducts internal surveys at least once each quarter, with ten to fifteen questions per survey. According to

Dave, Vietnamese employees are more reticent about providing frank feedback, so he uses these surveys to extract their thoughts. Finally, he also surveys his customers after every project. He wants to make sure that Vinasource is delivering happiness to them and that they are more than satisfied.

Localized Learnings

As a foreigner running a business in Vietnam, Dave has experienced his share of highs and lows. Throughout the process, he's learned a tremendous amount and adapted his Western-leaning management and leadership style to Vietnam. He shared the following insights:

- **Perception Matters**—Dave was used to working in spartan startup environments in the U.S. and carried that frugal mentality to Vietnam. In fact, his first office in Saigon also doubled as his residence and company cafeteria, too. Today, they've moved into a fabulous new building with a much better "address." He discovered that not only do his employees enjoy the extra "face" they receive when handing out their business cards, but even his employees' families are more boastful and happy.
- **Individual to Collective Bonus**—After Vinasource hit a goal, Dave gave everyone in the office a working day off. He thought that people would relax at home or run errands. Instead, when he logged onto Facebook the next day, he discovered that they'd all hung out together that day. So now, instead of an extra day off, Vinasource schedules a company outing instead.

- **Title Structure**—In the U.S., there's a lot of title inflation that Dave didn't love. He just cared that people got their work done on time. In Vietnam, workers are much more sensitive and attuned to their title, Dave learned. So he outlined everyone's title formally and introduced clear promotion paths.
- **Free Food and Drinks**—Most startups and technology companies in the U.S. offer free sodas and food to encourage people to stay and work longer. Dave has incorporated this into Vinasource. They offer free sodas, beers, and lunch on Friday. These perks are just as effective in Vietnam as anywhere.

Delivering Happiness

When Dave first read *Delivering Happiness* by Zappos' Tony Hsieh, he was so inspired that he had his management team read it, too. After they all read the book, they collectively changed Vinasource's mission to "Deliver happiness to clients and the team." Consequently, they try to relax and have more fun at work, which Dave notes creates a different ambience than the standard, rigid Vietnamese company vibe. He's introduced a popular foosball table recently, too.

To ensure that they are delivering happiness to clients, Dave leverages the aforementioned customer surveys to gauge how well they are doing, which measures the project team's accountability to their stated company mission.

Balance Fun with Accountability

Dave balances fun with a higher level of accountability for each staff member. To illustrate, Vinasource provides free

English lessons to the staff, and the team even plays Pictionary as a fun way to learn English vocabulary. Yet the company also administers tests to see if the employee's English is actually improving, which holds them accountable.

Avoid "Hit and Run" Initiative Overload

Many entrepreneurs go through this drill: they read an amazing management book, go to a conference and get totally fired up, or in some other way get super-inspired and then unleash a flood of initiatives to improve their business. Dave used to do this at Vinasource. He calls it a "hit and run" management style.

Today, Dave's mind still brims with ideas and initiatives, but he now limits initiatives to a maximum of two at a time— one that can be spearheaded by him, and one that can be spearheaded by his co-founder. This has resulted in increased company buy-in, change, and results. Dave's experience reminds us entrepreneurs to let off on the gas sometimes and tap the brakes instead.

Evolve Your Review Format to Get More Out of It

Dave has created the most comprehensive and dynamic review process that I've come across so far. It's quite detailed, so I'm breaking it down to the three main components below.

a) **Monthly Reviews**—Each team member who is working on a client project receives a monthly review that has a bonus attached to it. First, the entire project team receives a rating. Second, the individual will also receive a personal rating. Third, the manager will assign an overall project/progress rating. Fourth, they incorporate client feedback into the review. Everything is graded on a 1 to 5 scale. In order to receive a bonus, the overall grade for the individual must average 4 or higher.

Dave implemented monthly reviews because he realized that his team needed immediate feedback in order to improve. He tried many review formats before evolving into the system that Vinasource uses today. This format satisfies the need for timely feedback plus it ties in a bonus that can be up to 20 percent of an employee's salary, which is very meaningful. Because the bonus is so significant, his staff has become very focused on improving their ratings and pro-actively seeking feedback when they fall short. Dave welcomes and enjoys these conversations because he can now share his perspective and help employees understand how and where they need to improve.

b) **Semi-Annual Review**—These reviews affect bonuses and in rare cases are also an opportunity for promotions. This review is less project-focused and more development-focused.

c) **Annual Review**—These yearly reviews affect salary raises and promotions. Like the semi-annual reviews, these are also more focused on accomplishing individual milestones. Since much of the heavy lifting is done at the monthly project-based level, this meeting can be relatively easy, since the monthly reviews just roll into the big one at the year-end.

Conclusion

As our interview concluded, I leaned over and asked Dave Hajdu, in hindsight, if he should have teamed up with a local Vietnamese entrepreneur when starting Vinasource to avoid growing pains. Dave paused for a second, and then stated that he felt like he needed to make his own mistakes, because a local partner would have focused on micromanaging the staff instead of producing the great blend of East–West culture that they've created to date.

As I sat back, I was reminded of Dave's early revelation that working for someone else "sucked." From these experiences, I believe that Dave has created an environment at Vinasource that doesn't "suck" for his workers, but is actually empowering, fun, and meaningful to him, his staff, and his clients.

REMEMBERING VIETNAM

Vietnam brought back good memories. I was first introduced to Alice via Facebook when I'd visited Dave before in 2009. Coming back to Vietnam also freed me in a few unexpected ways. For starters, I could finally access sites that are blocked in China, like Facebook, Gmail, and Dropbox.

After traveling with three others in such tight confines for months, traveling solo was a nice break. Dave and I could stay out late or I could wake up later than 7:30am, when Keira always seemed to wake us up. As I was with Jeff, I was pumped to share with Dave my idea for a new company, thoughts that had developed since our time in Queenstown. He provided two additional lenses to help me evaluate the idea.

First, he admitted that he lacked a sense of how well Vinasource's culture is working. He thought this issue impacted him acutely, due to the reticence of his Vietnamese employees to open up to their bosses. One toxic employee can poison the work environment for others, so why wait for the problems to come out in the annual review season?

Given the culture in Vietnam, his "open door policy" was effectively a "closed door policy" in the eyes of the staff. Saigon, like many other places, is critically short of software developers. Dave dreaded receiving sudden resignation notices from his staff. Finding and replacing departed employees took precious time and money.

Hence, in order to retain employees, Dave and his managers need feedback. He wanted to know when his initiatives made employees happier, since they spend over half their waking hours at work. He didn't want to fly blind any more.

Second, he says I came to him like a changed man, brimming with energy around this idea. He could feel my passion about helping other entrepreneurs create happier workplaces while also recognizing the large market-size opportunity, since all organizations theoretically want higher morale.

TINY Beginnings

Dave also told me that for an offering like this, he'd pull out his credit card and pay immediately. We then began to talk about execution. After a deep dive into details, he became so excited that he offered me a discount for Vinasource to build the prototype if he could be a beta customer. Deal!

He needed a name for the project. I chose "TINYpulse." I chose the word *tiny* to bake lightweight, easy, and approachable qualities into the brand. We're not "huge pulse"—that is, we're not trying to be all things to all people.

I chose the word *pulse* because this service would send out surveys on a normal pulse-like cadence. Plus, it would give the entrepreneur the pulse on how his staff is feeling.

Finally, I chose to counterintuitively capitalize *TINY* because I felt that human resources often gets a bad rap. For example, when NetConversions was acquired by aQuantive and I had a question about benefits, my new boss told me to talk to HR. My visceral reaction was immediately negative. In time, I realized that Terry in HR was great and easy to work with. But why was my association with HR negative?

Most likely because in the past, I'd associated HR with rules, policies, and compliance. But I believe HR solutions done right can be elegant, positive, and tiny. That's why I decided to capitalize TINY: to reinforce the brand we're building.

Back on the Daddy Track

I look forward to returning to Vietnam someday with Keira and Alice so they can also enjoy the great food, massages, and Vietnamese culture (hopefully on a future careercation).

I returned to Shenzen, where Alice had been nesting with her dad, his wife, and their family, doing fun things like taking baby glamour shot photos. Kayla also took a much deserved solo vacation to explore Guilin and Yangshuo.

Alice's family relished getting to know our little Keira for the first time, and with delight and surprise they admired her independence and fearless attitude. They adored her and marveled at how she differed from their other grandchildren. For example, our bedtime routine is to finish with a kiss, put Keira to bed, and walk away. The other grandchildren's nanny was aghast that Alice didn't rock Keira until Keira was completely asleep or even sleep with her.

Alice enjoyed catching up with her family, but unlike Kayla and I, Alice hadn't had much solo downtime. So the hominess was starting to suffocate Alice. The lack of green space and being dependent on others for transportation only compounded the issue.

Leaving on a High Note

We decided that Alice needed some pampering. We let the grandparents look after Keira and treated ourselves to massages at a big, luxurious, Chinese-style spa, complete with TVs, cocktails, karaoke—and, typically, ashtrays.

On top of that, Alice's half-brother, David, arranged a big treat and helped knock off an item from my bucket list. When I studied at Peking University in the mid-90s, back when I first met Jeff Hu, I dove into Chinese culture. I started listening to Mandarin pop songs. My favorite singer by far was Jacky Cheung, a superstar then and now.

David mentioned that Jacky Cheung was delivering one of his final performances in Hong Kong. Were we interested in going?

Was he crazy?! Of course we were interested. I usually don't like concerts, but couldn't wait to see this one. Alice was excited too and recognized his popular hits. Almost two decades after I heard him on cassette tape (yes, I still have that tape), we got to hear him live, in person. It was fantastic to see fans from all walks of life and all generations come out to hear him sing. This was definitely a high note of my careercation.

⑥

Hong Kong

Moving the family from Shenzhen to Hong Kong was like flitting from one cozy nest to another, because Alice's dear aunt welcomed us to her Hong Kong home.

Alice enjoyed being around a familiar language, culture, and family in Shenzhen and Hong Kong. As a child, she stayed with relatives in Hong Kong during the summer. Those were magical times packed in her grandparents' house with other cousins from around the world.

A vibrant spirit of entrepreneurialism pervades the freewheeling yet efficient city of Hong Kong. Neon lights flicker through the night as the city throbs with energy and people.

For the record, Hong Kong was the easiest and cheapest place to buy SIM cards for our phone. Did I just mention *phone*? Funny how a few months ago I'd had phone and Internet withdrawal in New Zealand. Coming to Hong Kong, I felt the opposite. Now it felt like a nuisance to always check my phone for updates—I felt like a slave to technology, always checking for emails, calls, or texts.

On the interview side, I assumed that Hong Kong would be similar to my experience in Shanghai, but perhaps even more Westernized because of the British influence. The entrepreneurs I interviewed were mainly born in Hong Kong, and many were managing a family business, which I didn't experience anywhere else on my trip.

I had already started developing the TINYpulse prototype in Vietnam, but I was still anxious to see if its direction matched where these Hong Kong CEOs were going.

YUNG KEE:
The Goose that Laid Golden Eggs

Yvonne Kam

Yung Kee

Hallmark Cantonese restaurant, 200 employees, founded in 1936

Yvonne Kam is the third generation to run her family business: the world-famous, award-winning, foodie-renowned, iconic Hong Kong restaurant Yung Kee. Yung Kee has served up signature roast goose and Cantonese cuisine for seventy years. In 1936, Yvonne's grandfather Kam Shui Fai opened his first street stall, then moved into a commercial unit a few years later. That location survived Japanese wartime occupation, but not the air raids that followed, which led to a subsequent relocation, various expansions, and eventually a grand remodel of its current location on Wellington Street.

In 1968, *Fortune* magazine named the restaurant one of the top in the world, and Yung Kee has since been repeatedly recognized by many experts, from the local culinary reviewers of Hong Kong to Europe's most famous hospitality reference publication, the *Michelin Guide*.

When Yvonne came on board five years ago, she managed financial control and business operations. Her responsibilities increased when the restaurant's management transitioned from her uncle to her father.

Maintaining the thriving business meant that Yvonne had to bridge Chinese family business traditions with the modern-day expectations of customers and employees. Yvonne saw room for improvement—but improving processes and transitioning into the twenty-first century required change. How does one go about changing an entrenched seventy-year old company culture that has a life of its own?

It was bad enough that most operating procedures had gone unaltered for decades. Updating systems for managing the people who helped make the company great posed another dilemma. Many of the employees who have worked for Yvonne's family since its early years are still dedicated to the business. A lot of Yung Kee's distinctions are in its outstanding service. Never forgetting her deep roots, Yvonne recognizes the workers' unofficial tenure, and she manages them with respect and sensitivity. Yvonne shares her tips and tricks for improving Yung Kee's company culture while respecting old-school customs.

Strengthen Processes to Lay the Foundation for Culture

Old tried-and-true recipes are better for food—but not necessarily for operations. Yvonne inherited antiquated accounting processes when she started at the company. Every two weeks, the chief accountant would manually calculate payroll for two hundred employees. Granted, he used an Excel spreadsheet—but it didn't have any formulas. In addition, internal controls were lacking, and employees continued bad habits that had seemed okay for many years.

Yvonne overhauled the accounting department and focused on turning around the mom-and-pop shop mentality. In one instance, she went so far as to count Chinese New Year cakes in order to manage shrinkage and especially to send the message to staff that accountability is a priority. Yvonne leads by example, laying the foundation to build a better company culture.

Replacing Favoritism with Fairness

The loyal staff of Yung Kee is one of the restaurant's keys to authenticity and success, but this also has its challenges. Older employees have worked with three generations of the family, and each generation managed the restaurant in a distinct style. On top of that, the business switched from Yvonne's uncle's stewardship to Yvonne's father's in recent years, so another change of guard destabilized employees somewhat.

Some employees faced these changes with political games and manipulation in order to preserve their own standing in the organization. New employees had a hard time surviving this game, and morale suffered. Workers either had to join in the backstabbing, or put their heads down and stay quiet.

The older generation of management would typically let these dramas play themselves out. Yvonne decided to put a stop to the toxicity. She wanted to take a positive approach, but an incentive program like Employee-of-the-Month, which might work at other companies, would certainly fail at Yung Kee's. The winner of such a contest would be bullied mercilessly and resented. Instead of playing on people's competition, she decided to develop employees without being confrontational.

> *I admire Yvonne's willingness to tackle this issue head on since it would have been so easy to espouse a "keep doing what we've been doing" approach. I'm sure she didn't win many popularity votes, but sticking with her conviction was the right business decision to make. At the end of the day, it's not a democracy, and leaders have to make tough calls.*—David Niu

Tweaking Incentives to Help More People Move Up

In order to improve retention and incentivize floor staff to go the extra mile, Yvonne started paying quarterly bonuses based on monthly performance ratings. Yvonne also enforced a new pay and promotion structure to help her staff— especially new and junior staff—thrive within the company. Before, junior staff had a hard time getting promoted at Yung Kee. Typically, staff members would have to wait for their manager to leave—not an enticing career path when the average staff stays over ten years. Now, all employees have the opportunity to get promoted, regardless of their manager's status.

The new structure was well received by most, and all new policies are thoroughly analyzed, implemented, and communicated with caution to avoid harming company morale. Older employees are sensitive to change, so Yvonne consistently reiterates job security, reassuring them that new policies are simply for the betterment of the company.

Bridging the Communication Gap

Aside from customer comment forms, Yung Kee doesn't have formal means of getting feedback from the employees themselves. Culturally, in Asia employees in lower ranks are highly attuned to the management hierarchy. Someone approaching a superior with a complaint or suggestion happens only rarely. If management knows what really goes on day to day, it's not because they are receiving the communication directly.

Candid responses would be limited even if Yvonne reached out herself, so she assigned administrative staff to make daily informal rounds, reaching out to everybody, starting with "How's your day going?" Based on this informal feedback, the restaurant management can react quickly to potential issues, which in turn signals to staff that these daily chats can make an impact.

Conclusion

Knowing what matters to her employees—job security, a career path, bonuses for recognition, company pride, and being heard—helps Yvonne improve her human resource challenges. She celebrates small wins because she recognizes that it takes time to change a company culture. Finding a way to get an older janitorial staff member to improve her methods is a point of pride—and it reflects Yvonne's broader mission.

Yung Kee celebrates great wins too. Shortly after I interviewed Yvonne, the restaurant was awarded a "Caring Company" recognition by the Hong Kong Council of Social Service and a ten-year Quality Tourism Services Merchant Recognition award.

Yvonne acknowledges that she is risk-adverse, careful, and patient. These qualities translate into a sensitivity that might be her own greatest asset to moving Yung Kee Restaurant from a mom-and-pop shop to a corporation that can hold onto traditions and core values while thriving for generations to come.

PACIFIC ANDES:
Room to Grow at the Family Table

Jessie Ng

Pacific Andes

Frozen seafood processor and wholesaler, 20,000 employees, founded in 1986

Jessie Ng is the youngest of six children and the only daughter of Mr. Ng Swee Hong. After the family immigrated to Hong Kong from Singapore, Jessie's father started Pacific Andes in 1986 as a small frozen-seafood trading business. China was just starting to open up trade to the world. The grassroots operation saw tremendous growth over the years, especially when the family moved into fishing and processing in order to gain full control of the "ocean to plate" process.

Listed on the Singapore Exchange in 2006, Pacific Andes brings safe and nutritious seafood to customers around the world. With twenty thousand global employees and close to $2 billion in sales, the company shows no signs of slowing down. Jessie Ng, together with her five siblings, manages the operation. She gave me tips on wrangling a fast-moving company culture in a high-growth enterprise.

DO Mix Family with Business

Jessie and her five brothers are all involved in Pacific Andes. The arrangement works because they each have responsibility for different areas of the business, and they keep the same goal in mind: the well-being of the company. They regularly hold forums to discuss issues, and this communication contributes to a unified company vision, even among far-flung sections of the company. The siblings all have an entrepreneurial spirit and flexible attitude that keep everyone in sync.

> *I've never let any of my family members invest in any of my startups. I didn't want to mix money, business, and family. However, my wife is very involved in the business. I think it's helpful that Alice and I have normal check-ins to discuss issues and periodically monitor our alignment on the company's vision, mission, and values. I still won't let family members invest their money, but now I'm more open to working with friends and relatives.*—David Niu

Foster Enterprising Employees

As big as Pacific Andes has become, the Ng family still operates at a fast clip, maybe because they run the company like a true family business, with each person juggling a couple of roles. Nobody has time to "hold the hands" of employees who need a lot of guidance. This need for self-reliant employees has informed hiring decisions. People who can't pick up the reins on their own don't fit into this culture.

Creating a Strong Structure to Grow From

When hiring, Jessie and the crew look for someone who is willing to perform the duties as outlined and more. They look for self-motivated people who are willing to move beyond their expected role.

After Pacific Andes implemented a proper HR department, the company had help in adding strict guidelines to job descriptions, which helped streamline expectations and accountability.

Letting Little Fish Grow into Big Fish

Because Jessie's team hires high-potential workers, commonly an employee hired for a specific position will evolve naturally into a different role, based on their strengths and talents. One of Jessie's employees started as a secretary at age twenty, became Jessie's personal assistant, then an assistant buyer, and eventually got promoted to be a buyer. Still early in her career, there may be more promotions to come for this employee. Giving opportunities to internal staff and promoting from within are big wins all around.

Bridging Oceans, Connecting Cultures

A company with over twenty thousand employees worldwide and distinct subsidiaries will surely branch out with subcultures. For a while, the Ng family let each one operate the way that it was accustomed to before being acquired by Pacific Andes. At first, nobody tried to change a new subsidiary's management style to match its peers in other subsidiaries.

This approach changed a year ago. The company created a management committee to hold a monthly videoconference with all company department heads to discuss day-to-day issues and find ways to work together.

These monthly meetings cover daily challenges, issues, performance, and operations; they help top-level executives understand how to successfully synergize the different fields with one another. Managers are invited to tour the China operations facilities. Instead of trying to replicate a company culture artificially, Pacific Andes accepts the differences among the groups and instead focuses on working together through understanding.

Let Your Hair Down—Or Not!

Some cultural processes can be bridged with communication, but sometimes you just have to let groups of people be themselves. Jessie smiled broadly when sharing about the annual party. They have parties in two locations: mainland China and Hong Kong. Taking the stage and putting on skits is a big part of the party in mainland China. The employees there make a huge effort to put on a good show; fully enthusiastic, they get involved in details and take advantage of this opportunity to shine and let loose.

In contrast, the Hong Kong employees are reserved and more professional about their party; they let the organizing committee do all of the planning. It feels more like a company party than a free-wheeling festivity, and that is how they want it. One style of party definitely does not suit all.

Conclusion

Even though Pacific Andes is at the top of their game, a humble Jessie Ng says that there is always room for improvement, and she knows that she has a lot of work ahead of her. The company has constantly moving parts and branches with lives of their own. Jessie, who comes from a big family with lots of ideas and energy, has clearly embraced diversity itself as an important ingredient to success and a valuable part of a unique company culture.

DH SHUTTLECOCKS:
The Business of Badminton

Duncan Chau

DH Shuttlecocks

Manufacturer of badminton birdies and related merchandise, 1,300 employees, founded in 1978

Duncan Chau's first job was working for the family business, Double Happiness Shuttlecocks Ltd. ("DH"), placing little stickers inside the badminton birdies that his father had been manufacturing since 1978.

Anthony Chau, Duncan's father and the founder of DH, was a banker who desperately wanted to switch careers. After sending out a thousand letters seeking opportunities, he found someone overseas who was having a hard time obtaining shuttlecocks. At that time, shuttlecocks were specialized objects typically manufactured in England.

Overcoming the bureaucracy that had made it historically hard do trade with China, Duncan completed his first deal. Anthony started making shuttlecocks on the mainland and cornered a fast-growing niche market. Subsequently, he built the first factory, purchased the top-tier RSL brand, and made manufacturing agreements for well-known brands such as Prince, Wilson, and Head. Since then, the company has grown along with badminton's ever-expanding popularity.

As a kid doing sticker duty, Duncan developed a sense of family responsibility and respect for the small efforts that go into maintaining a business. He went to England for school, worked as an engineer, and earned an MBA before coming back to Hong Kong to run marketing for DH.

Double Happiness employs thirteen hundred workers, around half of those in the factory. The headquarters are in Hong Kong, a key distributor is in Europe, and one sales office is in China. Before Duncan came on board, turnover was very high at 20 to 30 percent. He has managed to slash that in half and initiate additional growth strategies.

Here are a few of the things Duncan has done to evolve the company and keep DH on top of its game.

Catch a Tiger by the Toe, if He Hollers Let Him Go

To keep operations more manageable, DH had to minimize their sales force, so they streamlined down from four to two offices. Duncan compared managing the other offices to trying to put leashes on a lazy tiger and a wild horse. On the one hand, he struggled with a potentially volatile but ineffective relationship, and on the other hand, he was faced with an entrepreneur whose needs and desires were not compatible with the business. Cutting the two offices out was painful and expensive, but he is now relieved to have a relatively simple slate on which to revamp the company structure.

Hold Out for the Perfect Fit

He learned by letting go of the "wild horse" that hiring people for a niche-product company is difficult. Top-tier people come in with expectations outside of the company's scope of possibility. Now, DH looks for someone who will fit into their industry with the ability to grow into a manageable role.

On the flip side, Duncan won't be timid about firing people who are not right for the company. He is confident that sticking with your vision and taking risks will lead to amazing hires and unexpected surprises. "You will never really know," he asserts. "It's better to be dynamic about change, go with the moment, and make the best decision you can."

I was guilty of hiring people who weren't the best fit at NetConversions. NetConversions was a consulting intensive business, so whenever we won a large contract, we'd have to turn around and hire folks to staff up the project. (This is one reason why I want to work on a product-based company instead of a services-based company).

When we hired these extra folks, I will admit that I was desperate. In hindsight, we should've negotiated a gradual project start, offered bonuses for current staff to work more hours, or turn down the project. The collateral damage of one bad hire is immense. I think the right long term solution is to constantly network and build up a bench of strong candidates that one can tap into at any time. Always be recruiting!—David Niu

---

Hold Inclusive Strategy Summits

Duncan's solution for managing at a higher level is to host large-scale strategy summit meetings for the different levels of DH's thirteen hundred worldwide employees: one for international, one for mainland China, and one for Hong Kong. These summits allow him to take a step back and listen while his employees discuss new ideas. He noticed that some of the more conservative managers who are usually dormant and quiet were so enthused about having a platform that they couldn't stop talking.

What makes these gatherings unique is that Duncan also includes his top customers. They are surprised to get questions, but involving them in "Start, Stop, Continue" discussions generates priceless feedback. Another important aspect of these meetings for Duncan is being on the "outside" of discussions. He moderates the summit, which he feels opens people up to communicating freely. If he participated in the talks, the direction might go a different way, so he keeps to the sidelines.

Learn on Planes, Trains and Automobiles

Duncan also travels with his sales people, taking five-hour bus rides and basic, economical lodgings with them. He takes the time to do this not just to bond, but also because his sales people give him the best ideas they glean from being on the front-lines with customers. One such successful idea was to put a sticker with technical specifications on the racket so that when there's no sales person, the racket will sell itself. With a product that doesn't change very much, Duncan keeps a close eye on the evolving needs of his customers by keeping in touch with his employees.

Improve Conditions to Increase Retention

Factory employees process 1.5 tons of goose feathers per day with limited cooling and generally difficult conditions. Prior to Duncan's arrival at DH, there didn't seem to be a need for a "culture" at the factory. It was smelly and hard work, and Chinese laborers seemed to be just fine with the stability of a steady job. But their turnover was a high 20 to 30 percent, so Duncan realized that they needed to do something to retain their factory employees. So they improved factory site amenities, automating some processes in order to improve conditions and quality. I was surprised to hear that there are sixteen categories of feathers that were hand-sorted until the recent automation.

Making a "Work Family"

The company also celebrates special occasions with parties, carnivals, and trips. Duncan integrates office and factory employees at company events to create a tighter community, which helps with retention. Duncan talked about the Chinese New Year celebrations that his factory workers enjoy before they go on their two-week holiday. The employees like spending time together. Making the New Year event feel like a family celebration gives the workers a reason to return to DH after the holiday. And if they bring a friend to join the company, DH gives them a cash bonus.

Let Different Teams Use Different Styles

Duncan is a big believer in integrating employees from different departments together whenever possible, but admits that not every experience has been a hit. He hosted a combined strategy summit for the China and Hong Kong offices, which have two very different company cultures.

The Hong Kong office employees want more ownership and are proactive about generating new ideas and communicating openly. However, when the mainland Chinese team arrived at the summit, their manner was guarded. They focused strictly on receiving instructions. This attitude inhibited the Hong Kong employees, who suddenly became quiet, and the full-day agenda ended up being a three-hour event. Duncan couldn't sleep for a week, lying awake and analyzing what went wrong, until he realized that it all came down to culture.

Conclusion

Learning different styles and honoring different needs is the nonhierarchical management style that Duncan strives for. This idea reminded me a lot of Jessie Ng's experience, learning to honor the unique styles that her groups have in planning even the annual party.

As an entrepreneur and member of a family business, Duncan considers it part of his job to take out the trash and travel with his sales team in order to experience what they're going through. Working on the manufacturing end is only part of what he does; he also has the mission of building the brand and diversifying DH's offerings into shoes, clothes, accessories, tournament sponsorships, and everything else where you would see a world-class sporting good line involved. Getting in the trenches is where Duncan gets his ideas to innovate and build the company culture that he envisions, from inside to out.

SHE.COM:
Designing Culture

Derek Yeung

She.com

Online marketing channel for fashion and beauty-oriented brands, 40 employees, founded in 2000

She.com is an Internet media platform and design house focused on marketing women-oriented brands. Like the beginnings of every good Internet startup, Derek Yeung and his business partners went with their gut instinct and no business plan.

She.com's design focus grew organically from the start, when they outsourced development of the site. Usually designers and programmers work in parallel to develop a site. But for She.com the designer led the project and vision. Consequently, when the company formally hired programmers, the culture remained true to its design-focused roots.

When they launched She.com in 2000, there were already three or four players in the beauty and fashion space, and by the end of the year, She.com had at least a dozen competitors. By 2003, however, after the dot-com bubble burst, the only two companies in the sector remaining were She.com and Elle.com.

In Derek's own words, "We were very worried because when Elle.com came out, we thought we were just a bunch of fashionable guys, why would anyone stick with us? They are Elle, as in the magazine!"

Fast-forward ten years: Derek is breathing easier knowing that She.com is here to stay. So how did She.com become the last man (or woman) standing? He credits his team for their strong design focus and the company culture, which he gives a high mark compared to typical Hong Kong companies.

Digging a little deeper into how the company culture evolved over time, I found out that like most of us entrepreneurs who start something from scratch, Derek had to learn a lot of lessons the hard way. He'd worked throughout his career in very corporate environments, and now that he was in a place where he could spread his creative wings, Derek had to adjust his management style and loosen up a bit in order to get the most out of his team at She.com.

Derek has incorporated a lot of the professional tactics that he learned from the Entrepreneurs' Organization, which I'm also part of. His team works well together, communicating, bonding, and innovating. But Derek stops short of adopting the more radical American management styles that a U.S. tech startup might embrace. He is not ready to offer unlimited sick and vacation days, for example. Derek is experimenting with the amount of structure that creative thinkers need to be productive.

Here are some of the tips that have helped him to find his way.

Let Employees Do Their Job

In the early days of She.com, Derek was such a micromanager that he actually edited employees' outgoing emails into perfect English. Aside from the fact that this practice wasn't sustainable, he realized that he was holding back his team's ability to develop their best ideas.

Flexible Work Hours Have Two-Way Benefits

Derek knows that most designers would prefer to work in the middle of the night. Even his partner would show up at midday. So Derek gave up trying to instill a 9:00 am – 6:00 pm schedule and compromised by shifting work hours from 10:00 am–7:00 pm. But staff still came in late. Thinking that he needed to be inventive about enforcing the new schedule, he instituted a "late fee." What resulted was people walking in late—with cash in hand and a bad attitude.

Derek's designers argued that while the employment agreement might stipulate that you come in at 10:00 am, it also mandates a 7:00 pm closing time. So, if Derek required punctuality in the morning, they reasoned that he shouldn't expect them to stay late at night. Derek appreciates the designers' hard work and finally conceded that hard work compensates for a traditional structure. He has since relaxed how he views a work day's schedule.

Create a Tiger Team from Within

She.com ran into a "good" problem. They were growing at a fast pace and working so hard on customer needs that they had to prioritize the revenue-generating projects over the internal work of redeveloping their own website. This dilemma was kind of like a fashion model being in such high demand that she doesn't have time to update her wardrobe. She.com is a brand that caters to the fashion and beauty industry, a world driven by image. And in the online world, you have to constantly stay on top of the latest trends, or a competitor will leave you behind. She.com could not afford to let their brand languish and lose their audience. Social media facets of the site and dynamic mobile technology components needed renovating.

Derek got creative and culled a high-performer from each of the groups in the business to create a separate internal team that would focus on She.com. Initially, the management team put up a fight, as each department was losing a star. However, the other players on each team could then step up and take more responsibility. The internal team of problem-solving tigers has made really positive changes. Derek is happy with this decision.

Huddle

Twice a week at She.com, they have a huddle to quickly review top-line issues and goals and to touch base. The team does not sit down in this quick meeting but remains standing;

this keeps the meeting short and concise. In fact, the managers like the practice and have taken it to their own team meetings.

Creating Effective Reviews is a Work in Progress

On the other hand, Derek has not updated the review process, and the company is using a template passed down from a big conglomerate. As much as he might dread the review, he acknowledges that it's a good jumping-off point to sit down, have quality time with his managers, and chat.

Don't Wait for Formal Reviews to Get Valuable Employee Feedback

More enjoyable and relaxed are the chats that Derek has with his employees over smokes. They take cigarette breaks, but he partakes in a cigarillo. It's in these impromptu moments that he learns about what's going on and what ideas people have.

"As I age, so does my management team," Derek lamented. "They are not old, but there are generation gaps. The younger people that we hire need to be listened to. Talking about online media without communicating with the younger generation—you think you are in the game, but you are not!"

> I believe "Open Door Policies" are myths. For over a dozen years in all my past companies I've had only a handful of people walk through that open door. Instead, much of the feedback is through informal chats, formal 1-on-1s, and office gossip. Moving forward, this is definitely an area that I want to keep a pulse on because some of the best suggestions come from the employees who are closest to the problems and solutions.—David Niu

Conclusion

She.com separated itself from the pack early on with a fashion-forward aesthetic. They have stayed successful by continuing to be progressive in the online-media space. Incorporating progressive management techniques goes with successful online companies like matching belt and shoes. One step at a time, Derek is evolving his people-management style so that She.com can stay on the scene for a long time to come.

AGNÈS B. DÉLICES:
Finding the Sweet Spot

Baldwin Ko

agnès b. DÉLICES

Retail stores selling gourmet
chocolates, 80 employees
founded 2007

I was excited to interview Baldwin Ko simply because he sells chocolate. What's not to love about chocolate? I met Baldwin at one of his agnès b. DÉLICES cafes before visiting his corporate offices and touring his five-thousand-square-foot "kitchen."

Baldwin Ko graduated with a Master's degree in real estate in Sydney, Australia. He returned to Hong Kong to work in commercial real estate, managing two of the city's largest luxury shopping malls. It was a great opportunity, and one of the malls—the famous Festival Walk—was the biggest in Hong Kong at the time. However, after the Asian financial crisis gripped the entire region, most of the mall remained vacant after opening. Within one year, Baldwin managed to achieve 100 percent occupancy. At the turn of Y2K, the Internet boom infused life into the retail market. Soon after that, another crisis wiped out business like a bad virus. It was, in fact, the SARS virus.

Around 2003, Baldwin had to reconsider how to survive in an industry so vulnerable to crises and fluctuating markets. Looking at the situation analytically, he studied successful tenants and evaluated what factors had contributed to their industries' success. Jewelry was an interesting avenue to explore, but it demanded too much capital up front. Fashion was another option, but Baldwin observed drawbacks in that field as well. The chocolate business, however, had weathered the economic storms of Hong Kong—so much so that some of the bigger brands doubled in size year to year in spite of economic crashes, drops, and crises.

For a couple of years, Baldwin explored chocolate brands around the world, both big and small, considering which ones might appeal to the Hong Kong market. One of his retailer friends from agnès b. fashion was moved by Baldwin's passion for chocolate and invited him to approach the designer agnès herself for a crack at a business opportunity. Eventually, Baldwin received the license to sell chocolate under the brand. But what exactly did it mean to create a chocolate brand?

The agnès b. brand license was granted to Baldwin in May 2007, and the first store was scheduled to open that October. Five months before the grand opening, he had neither a concept nor chocolatiers. Baldwin hired top talent from a leading chocolate company who ended up bringing their own business philosophies and company culture along for the ride.

Baldwin characterizes the other chocolate company as packaging focused rather than product focused. They were accustomed to repackaging their chocolates with slight variations, and they ended up overlooking the quality, origin, and training behind the chocolates themselves.

It was plain to Baldwin that they were speaking different languages, and that the philosophies brought from the other company didn't jibe with the agnès b. brand. "If you are selling wine to a customer for a premium price, would you simply change the label on the wine to diversify your product?" asks Baldwin. He soon realized that he needed to be more intentional about creating an enduring culture.

Baldwin shared some insights into the process of transforming his vision into the day-to-day operations and long-term success of a chocolate company. He's experienced both triumphs and struggles, and considers many aspects to be works-in-progress. Culture is not plug-and-play: Like the appreciation for fine wine or chocolate, it's cultivated over time. Here's a look into Baldwin's experience.

Passion Sells

Baldwin emphasizes the importance of chocolate knowledge in his current initiative, from the executive level to retail sales and all the way to the customer. The retail manager he hired from agnès b. had a background in sales and revenue and did a great job at moving the product.

Ultimately, though, she lacked a passion for chocolate and overlooked the intangibles of what it meant to sell artisan chocolate. When Baldwin interviewed his front-line staff, he realized that there was a huge disconnect between the main office and retail sales, and his message was not being delivered to the customer. For example, why was a specific combination of nuts and chocolate created? Sales people needed that knowledge in order to answer such questions. Educating his team and customers so that they all have an understanding of and passion for chocolate became key to Baldwin's company culture. This approach also serves to reinforce his brand: he was willing to hire and fire by those values.

> *I had so much fun during my interview with Baldwin. We toured his stores, his chocolate factory, and did the obligatory taste test (yummy!). I think Baldwin hit the nail on the head when it comes to passion. You either have passion for the company and job or you don't. It's okay if you don't, but then it's not the right fit for the company.*
>
> *On top of asking candidates how they resonate with our values, I also dig into their passions. What do they like to do outside of work? What gives them energy at work? What drains their energy? And then simply ask them why they would be excited to come to work on a daily basis to delight our customers. I know I can't fake passion, nor do I want any employees to fake it either.*—David Niu

Break Traditions

In Asian culture, it's common for business owners *and* employees to hold their cards close. Baldwin realized that his managers showed up to company meetings to just passively listen to him talk. Surprisingly, one of his managers even thought that if she didn't speak up, then no one would intrude on her department.

It took him a few months to readjust employee attitudes. They started to actively bring issues to the table and began resolving them with support from one another's departments. Recently, Baldwin started sharing company financials with his key managers. He hopes this empowers his staff with a sense of ownership and accountability towards the healthy overall growth of agnès b. DÉLICES.

Invest in Your Employees

Now that agnès b. DÉLICES has reached a certain level of success, Baldwin can focus on grooming his employees. His performance-review process takes employees' self-evaluations and in turn asks them tough and straightforward questions, such as: "what are your current and future achievements? How have you trained your staff better? Are you happy in your role?"

Baldwin deliberately makes himself approachable and encourages honest dialogue to spark change and improvement. The company's retail employees are receiving more in-depth training about chocolate and how it's made. Corporate employees are visiting the retail stores and receiving training that is more professional. Baldwin makes personal enrichment a part of his company culture, rather than just something that is nice to have.

Conclusion

Baldwin admits that he's still evaluating and re-evaluating his company culture, and constantly adjusts the magic recipe towards attaining ultimate company success. I discovered that the agnès b. DÉLICES brand, chocolates, and company culture all have a complexity and sweetness that didn't come about by accident. Baldwin struck me as a cross between Hugo Boss and Willie Wonka, bringing a blend of wisdom, fun, sophistication, and creativity that is reflected in the candy delights of his entrepreneurial dreams.

RED WOLF AIRSOFT:
A Marksman in Business

Paul Chu

Redwolf Airsoft

Online retailer and distributor
of airsoft guns, 40 employees,
founded 1998

"What is your favorite gun?" is a question that I never thought I'd ask during one of my careercation interviews. But that's exactly what I did ask Paul Chu, founder and CEO of RedWolf Airsoft. For those who don't know (including me, at the time), airsoft guns are highly realistic replicas that run on batteries, springs, and compressed air, capable of shooting up to forty pellets per minute. Some run on car batteries and can shoot upwards of six thousand rounds per minute.

It's like paintball, but since you're shooting a plastic pellet instead of a ball of paint, it travels farther, strikes more accurately, and YES—it hurts like hell when you get hit!

Paul started playing airsoft in 1996 as an escapist hobby. He quickly realized that there weren't any e-commerce sites selling airsoft-related merchandise in the United States, so he founded RedWolf in 1998.

Today, RedWolf distributes and retails premium airsoft war game products globally.

Paul, a former Andersen consultant with an e-commerce background, teamed up with Chris Pun, an airsoft expert. They've been partners for the past fifteen years, and they're learning how to meld Paul's Western management style with his partner's Chinese management philosophy.

Paul and Chris have managed to successfully grow the business, with more than forty employees in London and Hong Kong. But like any venture, it's seen its share of ups and downs. The following are lessons that Paul shared around leadership, culture, and people management, especially when balancing a Western/Eastern management approach.

Alignment of Company Culture Starts at Top

Paul readily admits that he's different from his co-founder, Chris. Paul describes his partner as more operations-based, whereas Paul is more sales-based. This difference rears its head when Paul tries to reset the company culture. Paul compares the quest for ever-elusive compatibility in business partnerships to seeking a spouse who has similar ideas on how to raise a family. Paul realizes that if he and his partner don't agree about the culture, it's very hard to disseminate consistent culture within the firm. That is his biggest challenge.

Be Patient for Improvement

In spite of management differences at the top, Paul candidly assessed that the company culture has improved from an "F" to a "C" in about a year. He is determined to keep raising the bar. Of course, such results rarely happen as fast as we entrepreneurs want them to.

Paul's recent initiatives are showing positive results, such as monthly all-hands "town hall" meetings, social gatherings where everyone can speak freely after bonding over beers or wine, monthly leadership meetings, and 1-on-1s with employees. Training his partner in this new, inclusive, open communication style is taking as much effort as guiding his employees in these practices. Nevertheless, Paul sees positive results and keeps finding creative ways to get his message across.

Let the Personal Bleed into Professional

Revamping the company culture has not been a one-way ride, with Paul evangelizing Western styles of working to traditional Chinese people. In reality, he thinks that traditional Western management compartmentalizes emotions and separates the personal from the professional. But he doesn't think that's a viable approach in Hong Kong.

To illustrate, a key employee is going through a divorce, so he's missing work. Paul has learned to be more flexible with him and has said to him, "Don't worry about it, I understand. Listen, you can just do stuff at night." The employee still cranks stuff out from home, and Paul supports an employee going through a rough patch.

Motivate Employees with More Than Money

Another time Paul realized that his approach needed major adjustment arose when Paul implemented an employee-incentive bonus plan. He meant to motivate his local warehouse staff with the bonuses. What happened surprised him. Acting insulted by his "stinking money," they were more concerned about *yi hei*, which loosely translates into a code of brotherhood, loyalty, and personal honor. This loyalty is earned by caring, not money.

To those staff members, "caring" means showing that Paul has *yi hei* for them. For example, he sparks passion and loyalty by rolling up his sleeves to help his warehouse staff pick, pack, and ship until midnight, rather than paying them a bonus. Nowadays, Paul is better able to motivate his team by understanding their intrinsic value compass; all of his Western training would have led him astray without this cultural sensitivity.

Eliminate Weak Links

Paul is a big fan of Cameron Herold's management tips. Cameron will ask a room full of entrepreneurs to raise their hands if they think someone within their company should be let go. Inevitably, a sea of hands goes up. Cameron then exclaims, "You guys are all chickenshit!"

Employers are afraid to let the weak links go because they don't think those employees can be easily replaced. But what about the cultural damage they inflict daily? No one is irreplaceable. What if someone quits or is hit by a bus out of the blue? As managers, we deal with those scenarios. Today, Paul identifies employees who are toxic to his culture and eliminates them as quickly as possible.

> *I think we've all had reservations about letting someone go. But what if that person decided to quit? The outcome would be the same. The person is no longer there, and you have to find someone else. Plus you're probably breathing a sigh of relief. As Cameron Herold says to people afraid to fire bad apples, "You guys are all chicken shit!"*—David Niu

Make the Most of 1-on-1s

Paul rated his company culture an "F" when team communication lacked quality. Meetings were generic. Now, Paul regularly takes his employees out for dinner to catch up. For these dinners, Paul brings his wife along and expects employees to bring their spouse, too. This creates an equitable balance and mutual respect. A happy side benefit: it humanizes Paul to the spouse, who then becomes more sympathetic when the employee has to work longer hours.

For meetings at the office, Paul has a special place set up in his office to sit comfortably, one on one, to catch up on matters that a Chinese employee would not typically open up about in a straightforward way.

Public Display of Performance

Paul maps on a matrix every employee's performance rating and their on-time rate (employees are expected to start at 9:30). A dot and the last four digits of their phone number semi-anonymously represent each person, so they can quickly recognize themselves and see where they stack up against their colleagues.

Seeing themselves ranked on the board shocked the heck out of many employees. Many didn't realize how poorly they were performing relative to others. Paul calls the lowest performing person "Bob." Of course, no one wants to be Bob. In the town hall meetings, people think, "Oh my god, I'm doing that badly. I didn't realize that everyone else was coming in on time." This public display of performance has resulted in immediate turnarounds.

Drawing a Line at the Top

Reviews are taken seriously and conducted twice a year on a very well-thought-out matrix that accounts for communication, being part of a team, performance, and attendance.

But with management itself being reviewed by staff in a 360 peer-review process currently championed by progressive management gurus, Paul's partner has to draw the line. In traditional Chinese top-down organizations, this loss of face would be totally unacceptable, inviting insubordination or an uprising!

Conclusion

Paul Chu is definitely a straight-shooter with tons of energy and classical entrepreneurial impatience. I can appreciate the challenges of balancing a culture constantly and slowly creating an effective blend of East-meets-West management style that works for RedWolf. It will be a constant effort, one I think Paul understands and embraces.

By the way, Paul's favorite gun is the P226 that John Travolta used in the movie *Face/Off*, and RedWolf was one of my favorite offices to visit.

WE'LL SEE YOU AGAIN, CHINA!

At a high level, it amazed me how much the locals embraced entrepreneurialism in Hong Kong. If you happen to start an online venture, the infrastructure there is outstanding. On our careercation, only Korea had faster Internet connectivity than Hong Kong. However, the taboo of failing in Korea dampens entrepreneurial endeavors.

Market size is another factor that supports new business activity. Hong Kong has convenient access to China and its one billion plus population. I won't be surprised to see a whole new generation of heavyweight online companies emerge from Hong Kong.

From my interviews, I noticed business leaders embracing new and Western-style management methods. At the same time, the Chinese sense of history and honor moved me, especially at family-run businesses. All of the entrepreneurs respected limits in their intents to move the business over to a "progressive" style of management. They understand that a culture will only bear so much change before people disconnect from it.

Whether an entrepreneur continued running the family business or started their own, I could see that people were still the root of pride and the cause of disengagement and heartache for managers. The themes I saw in previous interviews still came through clearly in Hong Kong. It deepened my dedication to offer a solution that can help leaders who care to make their employees happy—which will make the employers happy, too.

A Pause for Personal Business

After Hong Kong, we headed to Taiwan, where I was born. My dear cousin Jeff was getting married, and I would not miss it. I didn't schedule any interviews. I planned to just relax, hang out with family, and look forward to chowing on the world's best dumplings at Din Tai Fung.

Arriving in Taiwan was just as smooth as arriving in Hong Kong. Except this time, it was my family that welcomed us. My parents flew out for Jeff's wedding, and we all had a great time together. I also spent a lot of time with my cousins Eric and Teddy. Teddy's son is a little bit older than Keira, so I especially enjoyed connecting with him

With no obligations in Taiwan other than to relax, we finally had a chance to exhale and have fun. Like many of my Hong Kong interview subjects, my cousins all work at their family business. Hence, the wedding was a combination of business and pleasure on a large scale (a factory floor, to be precise).

As my relatives flew in from all around the world, they all had something to say about my decision to take time out of my career to travel. The reactions mostly reflected their ages. Older folks couldn't believe that we were still okay (especially me after my illnesses) and urged me to go home. Younger relatives were amazed that we pulled it off, and they peppered us with questions. Others, like my sister Ellen, could not fathom living out of a suitcase. "My shoe wardrobe is more than the two suitcases you guys lugged around," she quipped.

My parents loved hanging out with Keira and commented on her independence. It was fun to see her play with her cousin Jacob almost daily. Once again, she was adjusting to another country like a champ.

Kayla took vacation time for a solo venture around Southern Taiwan. My relatives were a little worried about her traveling alone since she didn't speak the language. But I reassured them that she was a seasoned pro by now. The only thing that dampened her solo trek was the pouring rain on her trip.

Crossroads

The wedding gave us a hard date to plan around, just like the EO conference in New Zealand. At this point in the careercation, Alice and I had arrived at a crossroads. We could keep the party going and explore Europe via Dubai, which I'd never visited and looked forward to checking out. Or we could head back to Seattle via San Francisco and Dallas to spend quality time with Alice's mother and my parents, respectively.

After much thought, we decided to head back to Seattle. Here are the factors we considered.

First, the health scare for Alice and me in Australia, plus the terrifying onset of Bell's Palsy in Korea emphasized for us the importance of health. One of the reasons I decided to take a careercation in the first place was to travel with my family while I am healthy. And after living in Asia's megacities without easy access to exercise and nature, we needed to go back and overbalance for health and fitness.

Second, Keira is an amazingly resilient and easygoing toddler. On our trip, she interacted daily with adults. But prior to our trip, she had both great professional educators and fellow toddlers at her daycare to socialize with. While our time together was precious, we also appreciate a more structured educational environment for Keira. We knew that returning sooner would mean she could have that again in Seattle.

Third, when I went to Vietnam, Dave Hajdu had helped confirm the validity of the idea that would become TINYpulse.

He'd also vetted the costs of developing the prototype. My interviews with Hong Kong CEOs further substantiated my belief that regardless of geography, industry, or organizational size, people need this management tool. By returning to Seattle, I could more easily focus on bringing the idea to market versus trying to coordinate software development while traveling from country to country.

Fourth, we had to admit that we were a bit homesick. It's nice to explore new cities, cafes, and local markets, but we also yearned to have a home base, especially for Keira. Additionally, Seattle in the summer is one of the most beautiful places in the world. That helped further sway our decision to come home.

Finally, the most compelling reason was that we now know that a careercation is not just a once-in-a-lifetime experience. Yes, it's nerve-wracking, scary, and intimidating to pack up and just do it. But now that we have done it, we know another big trip will happen down the road.

With proper planning, the rewards of a careercation far outweigh the costs. If it was our only chance at taking a big break, then we still may be traveling. But the confidence and beautiful memories of doing it once fortify our attitude that we can and will do it again. If we come up with a litany of excuses and are filled with anxiety—all the more reason to jump.

Good on Ya, Mate

It was now time to say goodbye to our au pair Kayla and send her on to Thailand, where she would meet up with girlfriends. After four months of constant togetherness, we were so sad to see her go! She was essential to our little travel team and we truly enjoyed our time together.

We witnessed how much Kayla had matured on the rip. Seeing her so homesick in the first few weeks but then watching her become an incredibly self-sufficient, self-assured, and capable young backpacker made us happy. It was similar to the joy I feel managing people who become successful. The end of our time together was bittersweet, and we feel lucky that she was part of our lives. We know that our paths will cross again.

Back in the USA

A bittersweet feeling washed over me when our airplane's wheel squealed upon landing back in the U.S.A. at San Francisco International Airport. After covering thousands of miles, conducting over thirty interviews, and creating an awesome collection of memories, our careercation was nearing its final chapters.

Alice's mom picked us up on a brisk, beautiful day in SF. My mother-in-law's trademark smile and laugh cemented the reality of coming back and nearing the completion of our journey. One of the first things I enjoyed was a long run in the fresh clean air. After Asia's megacities, I knew not to take public green spaces and clean air for granted anymore. On that same note, we decided to take Keira to visit U.C. Berkeley, where Alice and I had roamed almost twenty years ago.

It felt poignant to come full circle to our stomping grounds with a new family. Alice observed that the college campus had seemed so big when she was a student but now didn't appear that large at all. Time, age, and experience definitely altered our perspective. It was fun to see Keira running around Sproul Plaza and the big green space behind the library.

When weighing college options during my final high school days in Tulsa, Oklahoma, I did not enthusiastically enroll at Berkeley. I had doubts and didn't feel fully comfortable with the huge campus and large number of students. But like most things in life, including starting a business or taking time off to travel, I just had to jump. Within one month of arriving on campus, I couldn't imagine being anywhere else. Berkeley opened my eyes and my mind. Without coming here, I don't think I would've studied abroad for a year at Peking University nor would I have discovered the burning desire to embark on a life-changing careercation.

It was great to live with Alice's mother for a few weeks. She was amazed at how much Keira had grown and how much she could eat and speak! As for Alice, she loved our travel experience so much so that at night, she would discuss the merits of where our next careercation should take us. South America? Europe? Middle East? Or Asia again?

It's funny how we went from harboring so much angst at the start of our travels to even more angst at the end. We were already daydreaming about the follow-up hit! In our minds, another trip wasn't a question of "if," but "when."

Setting Mission and Company Values

If the next careercation was burning in Alice's mind, my mind was obsessed with TINYpulse. I decided that TINYpulse would be the first "TINY" offering that TINYhr would put out. I decided that TINYpulse's mission would be simply "To make employees happier." When that happens, magic occurs in the company culture.

I liked our clear mission, and now I wanted to set our company values. It came through loud and clear during my interviews that company values are essential underpinnings for a strong, robust culture. Furthermore, reading *Delivering Happiness* by Tony Hsieh also inspired me into action.

So I set out to be intentional about creating corporate values. In my journal, I wrote on one side names of all the people I've loved working with. I also listed why I loved working with them—their characteristics that stood out in my mind. On the other side of the paper, I did the opposite, listing names of individuals who drained my energy and whom I didn't enjoy working with.

On a separate sheet of paper, I outlined potential values for the organization. I then took these values and superimposed them on the people I loved working with first. I then asked, do these values enable these people to thrive? I also superimposed these values on the people who drained my energy and asked, do these values help weed out these folks? The first answer was no. So I edited and drafted new proposed values. I repeated this until the answer was yes on both fronts.

The following are the values we hire, fire, and make decisions based on:

D elight customers

E lect and spread positivity

L ead with solutions and embrace change

I ncrease communication with open engagement

G o the extra mile with passion

H old oneself accountable

T reasure culture and freedom

We made these values into an acronym to make it easier to remember. Today, we include this in all of our job postings (thanks for the tip Kwangsug) and ask interested candidates to provide two examples of how they've exemplified this. If they don't relate to these values or don't have the time to share, then I know they won't be a great fit for our culture. Better to get it out in the open sooner rather than later.

In fact, if the values of a business are crafted well and lived on a daily basis, then people will make decisions based on those values, reinforcing their meaning. As Andrea of Unimail shared, you can't just have values written on a sheet of paper and hung in the breakroom for people to look at without really knowing or understanding them.

Vision Impaired

San Francisco was a relaxing and welcome respite from being on the go. We had so much time to reflect and cherish our memories before embarking on the last leg of our careercation, which was a visit to my family in Dallas, Texas.

While in Dallas, I conducted one of my most favorite interviews with Ches Williams, the founder of Frontera Strategies. During our interview, he mentioned how he crafted his company's vision, mission, and values with the help of a renowned expert, Ari Weinzweig, a founder of Zingerman's Deli.

I had never heard of Ari, but after our interview I drove back and immediately devoured all of his writing and videos. In short, he helped me discern the difference between a company's mission and vision. For some reason, I felt great about our mission and values, but I didn't know where to start with our vision.

Ari simply states that the **mission** should be what the organization is trying to achieve. The **vision** should be what the future looks like if the company is accomplishing the mission. His exercise is envisioning himself five or ten years down the road in vivid, detailed "vision." He goes to great length to detail how the business looks, smells, sounds, and feels, in order to tickle and enliven all the senses. I loved it! I'm still not doing Ari justice, so please check out his site: www.zingtrain.com.

I now had my vision of where I pictured the business going next. I didn't include it here, since it's long and detailed, but I promise you that every detail that comes to pass at TINYhr helps affirm the big picture.

FRONTERA:
People Persons Helping People

Ches Williams

Frontera Strategies

Mobile medical diagnostic testing company, 60 employees, founded in 2001

Frontera is a mobile medical diagnostic testing company and was founded in 2001 by Ches Williams, Nate Nelson, and Richard Baker. They worked at the same startup fifteen years ago, and when the dotcom bubble burst, they were forced to figure out what to do next.

At the time, neither partner had any experience in the healthcare industry and didn't even get regular doctor's checkups. But they were intrigued with the space and had encouragement to pursue their business idea. Getting investors, in Ches' own words, was "comical" without any founder healthcare expertise, so they boot-strapped the business. They were able to get a small business loan, and the equipment manufacturer gave them favorable terms to start acquiring machines and diagnostic equipment. Today, Ches is happy to report that many of their first clients are still with them, and as Frontera's business has grown, so has that of their clients.

We dug more deeply into Frontera's growth and how their culture has evolved over the years. Ches often proclaims that he's no expert, but he shares a bunch of fundamental (and pretty damn good) best practices on how to improve company culture at work.

We're All in it Together

Looking back to 2011, Frontera went through tough times due to cuts from health insurance policies. During that period, they guarded information from others in the company. An epiphany happened at a low point when the founders needed everyone's help to turn the company around. Ches and his partners decided to open up a new era of transparency and shared financial data with key employees who had previously been in the dark about profitability and couldn't even guess the company's revenue size. They embraced the *Rockefeller Habits* company-wide, created quantifiable goals, and opened communications. Everyone got on board after this, and it became a turning point in the culture.

Integrate HR Earlier and with a Higher Purpose

Frontera hired their internal HR when they reached forty employees. Looking back, Ches wishes he'd hired an HR consultant much earlier on a fractional or retainer basis. Initially, Ches's partner did the HR, and he did not like doing it. But it wasn't any of the partners' core competencies, either. If they had brought someone in who knew what they were doing much earlier, they all would have experienced less pain going forward.

Hiring a full-time HR specialist brought a new, now integral energy to the on-boarding process for new employees. Frontera used to start new employees on Monday, the busiest day of the week, when managers were the most distracted. On top of that, new hires were relegated to a corner to fill out paperwork, then just lurked around until someone finally had time to focus on them.

Ches took an excerpt from a Jack Daly presentation:

Daly: "Show of hands, how many people have had a party for your employee on their last day of work?"

(Everyone in the audience raises their hand.)

Daly: "You're all idiots!"

Daly drives home the point that most company cultures do not invest in the on-boarding process as much as they should.

Ches and his partners decided to change Frontera's on-boarding process, and the moment they did, the employees loved it. From day one, a new hire starts to understand the company's history, vision, mission, values, and how the company makes money.

Now, newcomers have a welcome sign on the board with their name on it. On the first day of work, their coworkers have a party to show the employee that they're excited to have them on the team.

> *I like Jack Daly's question and have been guilty of this at NetConversions and BuddyTV. But now I see how important it is to make a first impression on new hires. Now I'm actively looking to upgrade our new hire integration process, especially their first week to focus on vision, mission, and values right away.*—David Niu

Recognizing What Motivates People

Ches acknowledges that they can always do better at understanding what motivates people. When a manager comes from a sales background, it's easy to assume that other people are also motivated by extra money. But Ches and his partners learned that some people want more recognition, others would like more time off, and some will strive a little harder to be rewarded with a trip. Ches aspires to create a compensation plan to help everyone achieve their goals, whatever they may be, and understanding the motivating factors is the first step.

Trophies for Winners

Every year, Frontera awards a "Heisman" award to an employee that goes the extra mile and embodies their culture. The idea behind this award: if everyone was like this prize-winner, Frontera would have an A+ culture. The award is a three-night stay with their spouse at a resort that Ches himself vacationed at many years ago. The experience at this resort left such a memorable impression that he still talks fondly about it today. He wants Frontera to have a similar positive impact on their own customers—he wants clients to talk about what a wonderful experience they had with the company's services.

You Got Caught!

Ches and his partners also know the power of daily recognition. His partner Richard started the "You-got-caught!" initiative that empowers employees to recognize their peers for good deeds each day. Many Frontera employees are field based, so the executive team rarely got to see them do phenomenal things. Employees feel great about recognizing a peer, and the peer loves being recognized. The initiative quickly gained popularity and effectively reinforces core values and purposes.

Take it Outside

In addition to daily recognition, Ches explains that company events are important unifying activities, especially because their employees are spread out over a large geographic area. "Frontera's Amazing Chase" was an urban race they personally created along with a hired event planner. It brought employees from different locations together in spirit. Everyone in the company knew that they were doing the same things as other employees in different areas, which built camaraderie and created a meaningful shared experience, which is vital to a positive company culture.

Speaking the Same Language

Frontera partnered with a company personality test called Culture Index (CI), which improves manager and partner communication with employees. Publishing the profiles company-wide promotes understanding amongst the staff. Ches now knows that he has to slow down when talking to someone in his office who is very detail-oriented, or use different listening skills with someone more introverted. The test results also assist in the hiring process. By better determining who will thrive in certain roles, top performers can be hired and nurtured more effectively.

Conclusion

For a guy who keeps saying he's not an expert in HR and company culture, he sure has a lot of great ideas. Ches acknowledges that with so many new culture initiatives coming down the pipe—Rockefeller Habits, You-Got-Caught, Culture Index, and a few more—Frontera risks overloading employees. People might just throw up their hands and say, "I don't get all this stuff!" So Ches intends to patiently see these things through and to let change happen over time.

He says, "The train has left the station and we're going down this path. It's up to us to help them believe it, but not everyone wants to be along for the journey, and that's OK."

Maybe the key is to admit we're not perfect so that we'll always keep striving to do better.

APEX FACILITY RESOURCES:
Swooping in to Help

Marlaine McCauley

Apex Facility Resources

Delivering innovative
workspace solutions, 75
employees, founded 1997

I love connecting with other entrepreneurs because
everyone has had their own unique path to success. For
Marlaine McCauley of Apex Facility Resources ("Apex"), her
"ah-ha" moment came in February 1997 when she was eight
months pregnant. She did a consulting project for King
County (where Seattle is located) for five hundred wall
panels. Marlaine recognized a niche opportunity for building
out new workspaces. She then went out and established her
own business account and business license with just $500 in
her pocket, and a business was born. Now it's fifteen years
later, and Apex employs seventy-five people.

The company is a one-stop shop for planning, furnishing, relocating, and expanding productive workspaces. Their menu of products and services enables customers to partner with Apex, get responsive and nimble service, and save the hassle of shopping with multiple vendors.

Marlaine shared some great people management tips.

Separate Performance and Compensation Reviews

Apex conducts performance reviews in June. Compensation reviews are done once a year in December. Throughout my career from Andersen Consulting (Accenture) to NetConversions to aQuantive to BuddyTV, we've always coupled the two reviews together. But I can definitely see the benefit of decoupling them so that the performance review really digs deep into performance without co-mingling with compensation implications.

Conduct Semi-Weekly 1-on-1s

Doing reviews frequently eliminates surprises to the reviewee and reviewer. In addition, the reviews all roll up into the annual review, making that process much more manageable and streamlined. In fact, Marlaine admitted that her annual review is actually easier than her 1-on-1s!

> *I know entrepreneurs often rush to the urgent at the expense of the important. So I commend Marlaine for sticking with her 1-on-1s, which not only give her a pulse on what's going on, but also make her annual reviews a breeze. I think a good way to keep the momentum and rhythm of these 1-on-1s is to just schedule them on a recurring basis in your calendar.*—David Niu

Helping Managers Help Others

Apex leverages an outside consulting firm to help them continue growing successfully. Everyone took a course from Performance Management Consultants, who provided particularly valuable guidance to managers on how to deliver a variety of messages.

Performance Logs Vital

The semi-weekly 1-on-1s use performance logs to focus discussions. Employees bring to the meeting a sheet with four completed squares that log and measure goals and achievements. Apex wants reviewees to take the first cut at the performance log so the employee will own their performance and improvement.

HR Compassion

No matter how hard you try, managing people still takes the most time and causes the biggest frustrations. It's just a very challenging task set. We'll never know everything there is to know. However, simplifying the process is huge for Marlaine moving forward.

Conclusion

I loved hearing how Marlaine stumbled into being an entrepreneur, and the opportunity turned into a seventy-five-person enterprise. She remains very grounded. I admired her honesty when she admitted that HR is challenging and frustrating, and that she'll never know everything there is to know about it. Nonetheless, she seems to have established a great review rhythm makes the big annual reviews relatively easy. Investing in chores regularly helps challenging tasks go more smoothly in the end. And just like Apex swoops in to help clients with the tough stuff of moving offices, bringing in outside help for developing managers has paid off for Marlaine and her company.

CHAMELEON TECHNOLOGIES:
Showing True Colors

Mike Luckenbaugh

Chameleon Technologies

Technical staffing and
professional services, 42
employees, founded in 2000

When I sat down with Mike Luckenbaugh, co-founder of Chameleon Technologies ("Chameleon"), he struck me as someone who is very likable and easygoing, which helps explains the success of his company. Chameleon provides consulting services, temporary staffing, and recruiting for some of the largest companies in the Puget Sound region, including Microsoft, HTC, and REI.

Chameleon undertakes strategic planning once a year in December and then reviews the goals quarterly to see how they're tracking. Mike shares the outcome of the strategic planning in a company-wide "State of the Union" address with the troops to get them rallied and on board. Mike discussed the following approaches to keeping his forty-two employees happy and committed to continued growth.

Leverage Employee Feedback in Review Process

Employees complete a form prior to their annual review. They document their successes, areas for improvement, and wins. Then management completes a similar form. During the meeting, they match the feedback from both sides and really dig in, especially in areas with discrepancies. The meetings usually take about an hour.

Quantitative Scale for Raise

Managers grade reviewees on a scale, then tally all the points. An employee must hit at least forty-five out of fifty points to warrant a pay increase. The qualitative feedback in the process is quantified for easier comparison and performance tracking.

Share the Spreadsheet Love

Mike is a self-admitted spreadsheet wonk. He tracks performance and productivity all via spreadsheets. And he leverages a corporate shared drive to share reviews and progress internally with other key members of his team.

Praise (a Lot) in Public

During their standup meetings, Mike often praises people in public. He's a big believer in giving people recognition and respect in front of their peers and the entire company.

> *Giving public recognition is so simple. But how many times in the past week have you given public recognition, especially to more than one person? Or given public praise to someone who is not a direct report?*
>
> *I know that whenever I provide public recognition, it sends a wave of positive peer-to-peer recognition throughout the company. As leaders, we should always aim to give recognition on a consistent basis to our direct reports and to those who aren't our direct reports. Give to get.*—David Niu

More is Better

Mike employs a monthly 1-on-1 meeting rhythm because he's able to resolve any issue quickly before it gets out of hand. For the 1-on-1, the reviewee fills out a form with eight different sections one hour before the meeting and sends it to Mike. They'll then sit down for about an hour—the duration of the review—to discuss all 8 sections together.

Conclusion

They say that companies embody the personality of the founders. If this is true, I can only imagine how much clients enjoy working with Mike and his team, given his amiable personality. But even with a friendly founder and work environment, there's bound to be anxiety and issues during annual reviews, especially when expectations don't line up. Therefore, I understand why one of the reasons Chameleon boils the qualitative feedback down into a quantitative points system is to depolarize potential conflicts.

AVIDIAN TECHNOLOGIES:
Trust in a Great Culture

James Wong

Avidian Technologies

CRM software developer, 34 employees, founded in 2002

James Wong of Avidian Technologies gave me one of the funnest interviews so far. James is educated as an accountant, trained as an engineer, and baptized an entrepreneur by fire. He started his first company, an ebusiness consultancy, at twenty-four years old and sold it four-and-a-half years later.

After reviewing the pros and cons of his first startup, he decided that he was "lazy" and didn't want to bill by the hour like he did with his first company. Instead, he wanted a business with leverage. So he started Avidian Technologies, a CRM software and product company with a co-founder Tim Nguyen in 2002.

Avidian's mission is to create an easy-to-use CRM software inside of Outlook. James observed that most people are in Outlook all day long. Who doesn't check their emails first thing in the morning and sneak in one more glance before hitting the sack? Since most salespeople spend 50 to 60 percent of their time in Outlook, it was an intuitive next step to create an easy-to-use CRM system inside Outlook that would spur adoption. He named it "Prophet," which is a tongue-in-cheek play off of "Outlook." Prophet distinguishes itself with better accuracy and farther future projection.

Today, Avidian employs thirty-four "associates." James insists that they not be called employees and that the associates leverage the five company principles to make decisions.

James shared a plethora of interesting insights on culture, HR, and performance reviews. Here are some of his best tips.

Big on Culture and Guiding Principles

He referred to this multiple times from the beginning of the interview to the end, so I know that he sincerely believes in building a positive company culture.

His Five Guiding Principles are a neat acronym, **TRUST**, which stands for:

Treat each other as we would like to be treated
Respect associates for putting family first
Uphold excellence in all we do
Share success with associates, clients & world
Treasure People by Promoting from Within

James proudly shared that he often overhears associates making decisions and invoking TRUST. Most businesses just pay lip service to these types of company pronouncements, so employees easily and forget about them, just as the founders do during day-to-day operations and decisions.

Rockefeller Habits

James leverages the approach espoused by Verne Harnish's *Mastering the Rockefeller Habits: What You Must Do to Increase the Value of Your Fast-Growth Firm*. I have to admit I'm quite a big fan of the *Rockefeller Habits* too. Avidian uses this philosophy for annual strategic planning, monthly GMTs (goals management team meetings), and weekly and daily meetings. One key takeaway from the *Rockefeller Habits* is that the faster your company is growing, the more you need daily meetings for alignment. This may be counterintuitive since most entrepreneurs dread meetings that waste time. Harnish preaches that if done correctly, meetings can be short, efficient, and beneficial to productivity.

Borrowing the Zappos Philosophy on Raises

Who cares if it takes someone six months or three years to master a skillset before they receive a raise? If it's faster, why don't we provide them a raise right then and there instead of waiting for a year or some predetermined HR review period? James uses this inspiration to motivate his staff and compensate them frequently in a less structured way than traditional annual compensation reviews offer.

Breaking Bread with Employees

James likes to take his associates out to lunch to just talk and listen. He views this as a casual, approachable way to learn what's blocking them from reaching their goals. Long gone are the days when management executives would have their separate executive-only dining area!

Polite About Feedback

During the interview, James brimmed with enthusiasm and excitement. He was quick to share feedback and elaborate. So when he said that he likes to ask associates if he can provide feedback, I paused, wanting to learn more. He often starts by asking, "Can I share something with you?" or "Are you open to a coaching idea from me?" Most of the time, the answer is "yes," especially with a softened start like this. But sometimes the answer is "no," and then he keeps his mouth shut.

Reasonable About Raises

When providing compensation reviews, he first looks at the performance of the company. Then he'll review what each associate wrote about his or her own performance and compare that to his thoughts. They'll fall into a range from exceptional to medium to poor (but Avidian really doesn't have these classifications at the company) before then talking about raises. He finds that everyone at Avidian has been reasonable with raises. And if there is someone who requests a number higher than the budget can accommodate, the company can usually find a way to offer that amount contingent upon the associate hitting a quantifiable goal to justify the additional increase.

Questions Value of Annual Reviews

At the end of the day, James fundamentally questions the value of annual reviews. He admitted that some years, he overlooked doing them. No company backlash ensued, and the business performed equally as well as the years that they did conduct reviews. So do reviews fundamentally have a positive, negative, or neutral effect?

> *I'm with James in fundamentally questioning annual performance reviews. I know there has to be a better way. I think we're going to start seeing new philosophies and approaches for more real-time reviews. I believe this is better for the reviewer and reviewee versus a mandated annual sit-down.*—David Niu

Conclusion

For all the energy that James exhibited throughout our interview, his parting thought was the most provoking: "Do we really need annual reviews?" Because if the reason is a compensation review, why don't we just schedule compensation reviews and do rolling performance reviews throughout the year? Or is there a way to be like Zappos, who does rolling compensation reviews along with rolling performance reviews? Ultimately, James is an ardent believer in human capital and getting the best out of people. He reads a tremendous amount on this subject, and similar to Marlaine of Apex Facility, I don't think we'll ever know all there is to learn about HR and managing people. But clearly, implementing proven best practices espoused by Tony Hsieh and Verne Harnish is a great place to start building a positive culture with clear values.

WETPAINT:
A Fresh Approach

Ben Elowitz

Wetpaint

Entertainment news
publisher, 45 employees,
Founded in 2005

Every now and then, I get fired up and inspired by someone I'm interviewing. Ben Elowitz of Wetpaint falls into this category. Ben started Wetpaint in 2005 with seven other people, and he freely encouraged all of them to think of themselves as co-founders.

At first, Wetpaint's goal was helping people create all types of content online as the whole world was going social. Now, at forty-five employees, Wetpaint is focused on how people are distributing their entertainment and celebrity news via Twitter, Facebook, and the like. Ben Elowitz categorizes Wetpaint as a next-generation web publisher, like *People* or *Entertainment Weekly* (Wetpaint was recently acquired by Viggle, over a year after this interview was conducted).

When I spoke with Ben, they were doing operating and financial planning in November and December. They also performed a mid-year checkup, gauging initiative performance, new lessons, and necessary changes. As systemic as this may sound, they are definitely not afraid to switch things up outside of these cycles.

To keep himself accountable, Ben's board of directors helps him examine the facts. They also host a two-day board offsite to become realigned every year, which Ben finds amazingly helpful. Now that the company is firing on all cylinders, they hold less frequent, less intensive board meetings.

Ben is very introspective when it comes to best practices around people management, leadership, and culture. The following are his experiences around these issues.

Weekly 1-on-1s with Top Fives

For his four direct reports, Ben conducts weekly 1-on-1 meetings. Everyone has a list of the top five things they're working on, as well as things they need from him. Feedback is exchanged both ways. Ben finds that this process keeps everyone focused and accountable.

Performance Review as Meta-Goal

Ben thinks that performance reviews are "important, life-changing, inspiring, lots of work, and hard to teach." Most employers don't share this enthusiasm, so I was immediately eager to learn more. In his view, the goal of performance reviews should be to quickly move people very far forward in their careers. Reviews can, in his view, serve as a valuable once-a-year opportunity to inspire and tell people how far they can go, not just in work, but in their lives. Ben's best managers always made sure he was getting better and better every year, and he strives to do the same for those that work with him.

At the same time, he hopes that the reviewees think of the annual review as he does. He concedes that regardless of how much he evangelizes progress around reviews, people probably still fear and dread them.

Separate Performance and Compensation Reviews

Performance and compensation may be measured using the same process, but in separate meetings. The performance review is done first, and the performance score is a big part of their compensation review.

Ben likes separating these two discussions because most of the time the reviewee fixates on "the number" of the compensation review. In Ben's mind, reviews should be 70 percent professional development and personal growth and only 30 percent performance assessment.

Internal Review Infrastructure

Wetpaint invests in teaching managers how to better conduct reviews. They focus on positioning the review as a true opportunity to improve the professional development of the team. He feels that if he doesn't train his managers, they'll simply fill out a form and be done with it.

No Surprises Mentality

Ben believes ardently that nothing should come as a surprise in a review. Feedback should be provided on a rolling basis, not saved for later.

Calling BS for More Candid Feedback

During 360s, if someone gives a peer or manager all fives, Ben will send the form back. He'll remind them that this process is about helping people become better, and that they need thoughtful feedback on improvement. Only honest, critical feedback moves people forward.

> *Ben was so genuine during the interview, and I believe in his well-meaning intentions to dig deeper for constructive feedback. Every reviewer and reviewee needs to keep in mind that it's easy to just fill out some forms, but it's much harder to uncover true opportunities for improvement. Those prospects are gifts that management can provide, as long as a plan to address those opportunities is created along with the employee.*—David Niu

Ben's Personal Four-Quadrant Review Process

Ben's accountable for four annual reviews. He spends four to six hours on each. He starts by dividing a sheet of paper into four quadrants:

- What went well in terms of results?
- What went poorly in terms of results?
- What are the individual's strengths?
- What are the individual's areas for improvement?

Then he fills out each quadrant with a bulleted list. He also considers the input he receives from 360 reviews (each person has three) and the reviewee's own self-assessment. He analyzes this and then lists, at the top center of the sheet, three top priorities for feedback during the meeting. He calls this his "MIT" for "most important thing." Otherwise, giving feedback on everything is too paralyzing, especially if there are forty or fifty bullets to go through. Ben admits that this is thorough, but he wonders if it is too thorough.

Conclusion

Ben shared many nuggets and tips on conducting performance reviews, but most refreshing was his philosophy that reviews are a formal once-a-year opportunity to inspire and move people as far and as quickly as possible at Wetpaint and even beyond as individuals.

I'm a big believer that we have a choice when faced with any situation. We can have a positive, neutral, or negative attitude, like "Today's going to be a great day!" or "Work's going to suck today." And to some extent we do attract what we think. The kicker: the mindset we choose is free, so why not be positive or at least neutral?

Even though he admits it's hard and takes him up to six hours per review, Ben adopts a mentality of "important, life-changing, and inspiring," a good reminder of the opportunity and obligation all entrepreneurs and managers possess.

YOOGISCLOSET:

Window Shopping Pays Off for Simon Han

Simon Han

Yoogiscloset

Authenticated pre-owned luxury goods online, 12 employees, founded in 2008

For Simon Han, window shopping really paid off, sparking his "ah-ha" moment to start Yoogiscloset. Simon was vacationing with his wife, Eugenia Han, in Japan, checking out the various shops in the fashionable Ginza shopping area. Simon noticed that the side streets were loaded with consignment stores.

Not dumpy, attic-smelling thrift stores, but extremely high-end stores that mimic the feel of an actual Louis Vuitton store. On one side street alone, Simon counted ten to twenty high-end stores selling pre-owned handbags. That's when inspiration struck: how about a business to start an online version of shops that buy and sell pre-owned luxury goods?

Upon returning to the U.S., he dove into researching the idea. At first, Simon was hesitant to start a business with his wife. He'd heard all the horror stories of how working with a spouse can create major friction in a marriage. He took all the advice in stride, plowed forward, and has never looked back with regret. It's been all good between the two of them, and Eugenia's nickname "Yoogi" sure sounds better than Simonscloset, which has a creepy feel (in my humble opinion).

Yoogiscloset employs twelve people and is now the leader in the online space for buying and selling pre-owned, authenticated luxury goods. Simon firmly believes that they do the best job of sourcing goods. He's streamlined the procurement process into a competitive advantage. Another point of pride is Yoogiscloset's unblemished track record of never selling a single counterfeit. Allowing even one would kill client trust.

The high level of authentication does slow down the sales process, but the tradeoff is non-negotiable. Simon sees fakes on competitor's sites, and he is not willing to risk Yoogi's trusted brand.

Simon was not a stranger to starting up a company before Yoogiscloset. He started CarDomain Network, Inc. in the late 90s, which enjoyed phenomenal growth along with the evolution of the Internet and social networks, and his former company continues to do well. Simon's experience at

CarDomain has informed his leadership style at Yoogiscloset. Here are some tips he shared with me.

No Surprises

At CarDomain, Simon was shocked when an employee was caught completely off guard by something in his performance review. Simon thought to himself, "What's wrong with this person? Do they really not see this?" But now he realizes that blindsiding his employee meant he had goofed as a manager. Now, Simon delivers constant informal feedback and believes there should be no surprises during the annual review if the manager has properly done their job throughout the year.

> *I like surprises in many contexts, but I despise them when it comes to evaluating performance. If I've done my job as a leader, then my team should know exactly where they stand. No surprises. And it should be mutual.*
>
> *In fact, when we do contract-to-hire agreements, I always ask at the end of each month, "if your contract were to end today, would you be all in?" This provides me a good pulse on where the candidate stands. I will also answer the same question, so that the candidate knows if they have my full support and enthusiasm. Always err on transparency.*—David Niu

Linking Performance and Compensation Reviews

At Yoogiscloset, performance and compensation reviews are linked together and conducted in one meeting. However, CarDomain management separated reviews by several months since they conducted a lot of peer-on-peer 360 reviews. This separation engendered better peer feedback during 360s. The time interval decreased the perception that meaningful constructive feedback would ding the person during the compensation review. Simon decided to combine them at Yoogiscloset because with only twelve employees, it's more manageable to integrate the two. Plus they do not conduct any 360 peer reviews.

80/20 Breakdown

Eighty percent of the annual review meeting focuses on results of the past year, and twenty percent is allocated towards goal setting for the upcoming year.

Meaningful Upward Reviews

Simon was challenged with upward reviews while at CarDomain. How can one provide anonymous upward feedback and include detailed examples? Answer: bring in an outsider. The consultant interviewed Simon and all the VPs. Then the consultant delivered the upward feedback to the CEO. Simon found that talking to the outside consultant helped depolarize the situation and made people feel more comfortable providing candid feedback on their boss's performance.

Conclusion

Many fast-growing companies, claiming to be too busy growing, elect to skimp on performance reviews. But after window-shopping management styles, Simon has adopted the best parts of the performance review process from CarDomain and customized them for Yoogiscloset. He combined the performance and annual reviews since his company is smaller, yet he stripped out the 360 peer-review assessments since they are very time-consuming. At CarDomain, some managers would do ten performance reviews at a time. I look forward to seeing how Simon continues to adapt his review process as the company grows.

GROUNDSPEAK:
A Hidden Seattle Success Unearthed

Jeremy Irish

Groundspeak

Inspiring and supporting outdoor play using location-based technology, owner/manager of Geocaching, 70 employees, founded in 2000

For the first TINYhr interview, I had the pleasure of sitting down with Jeremy Irish of Groundspeak. Groundspeak is one of the most successful and influential Seattle companies a lot of people have never heard of. If you've ever gone geocaching or heard of someone who has, you can thank Groundspeak, which is the parent company of Geocaching.com.

If you haven't been initiated into this addictive pastime, geocaching is a real-world, outdoor treasure hunting game using GPS-enabled devices. Participants navigate to a specific set of coordinates and attempt to find the geocache container hidden at that location. There are geocaches hidden worldwide.

Jeremy first started Groundspeak in 2000 as a hobby with the goal of getting people outside. He wasn't in it for the money. When traffic to the site exploded, he incorporated the company, fearing lawsuits if someone twisted an ankle or got lost while searching for a cache.

He first named the company Grounded Inc. to remind people associated with the company to remain Earth-bound. Plus, the prizes were hidden on the ground. This culture of groundedness and humility really came through in my conversation with Jeremy. Everyone in the company is called a "lackey" because their goal is to serve their burgeoning community of enthusiastic users. To further embody this culture, the company's first furniture was purchased from failing dot-coms in an effort to remain frugal.

The company has grown to seventy employees, and Jeremy shared some of his top tips and hard lessons learned, including:

Provide Compensation BEFORE Performance Review

Jeremy's reasoning for the unique choice of providing compensation reviews before measuring performance is that everyone just wants to know the number during the review. Why not hand them the number first and get that out of the way? Then the real review begins.

An Ally in Self-Assessments

Having employees assess themselves is a useful process for managers who conduct reviews. They also provide an opportunity for the employee to be heard. Jeremy doesn't sense that self-assessments are unfair or skewed. On the contrary, he's impressed by how critical and balanced the reviews are. Maybe this sprouts from the culture of humility?

1-on-1s= Weekly Rhythm

Jeremy established a tempo of weekly 1-on-1s with his three direct reports. These typically last thirty to sixty minutes and provide a venue to share what's going well and what's blocking them. He's heard very enthusiastic feedback from reviewees, who thank him for a structured 1-on-1 instead of just a casual conversation.

HR at 50

Groundspeak hired their first full-time HR person when they hit fifty employees. Now they have two full-time HR employees. These folks make sure that reviews are conducted and also archive and store them.

Culture, Culture, Culture

Jeremy referred to culture quite often during our interview. He thinks that every company should name or brand their team members. Similar to how Yahoo has "Yahooligans" or how Groundspeak has "Lackeys." This rallies people and reinforces the culture.

> *I love Jeremy's focus on culture. "Lackeys" is such a great term since it connotes service and humility to his clients. I think I'll need to get creative to come up with a team brand that embodies our vision, mission, and values. Then it'll become another addition to our company brand and lore that I can add to make the job req, interview, and onboarding even more robust.*—David Niu

Conclusion

I came away very impressed that what was only a hobby in 2000 has grown to a seventy-person success story in a dozen years. I'm amazed at how critical people are of themselves during the review process, since most people are actually concerned about the opposite effect. Few people know the trajectory that Geocaching.com has been on, or that it's based in Seattle. I think that's just the way Jeremy and the company of humble lackeys like it to be.

WRAP UP

Planning our return to Seattle, we had to determine where we were going to live. Since we had earlier downsized and sold most of our possessions, we were basically living out of two large suitcases, even after the trip. Given that, we decided to move into Alice's downtown one-bedroom condo. We thought if we can live out of our suitcases, a condo must be luxurious!

Keira liked the location too, because it was right across the street from a fun park and walking distance to the Seattle Children's Museum. Alice liked not having to pack and unpack constantly, instead having a permanent place to call home. Plus, she welcomed all the easily accessible organic fruits and vegetables available in Seattle. Personally, I loved the condo's close proximity to the waterfront. It motivated me to get out and take care of my body with runs along the water. As I had learned, I had to invest in maintaining my health and couldn't take it for granted.

The condo had super-fast, free Internet in the lobby. I was jumping on Skype chats there with David in Vietnam, talking about the progress of the prototype that would eventually become TINYpulse. Since I was so committed, I decided to bring on a local developer to accelerate progress. His name is Zach, and he helped launch the beta version of TINYpulse from our condo lobby.

It's the People, Stupid

Looking back on all of my interviews, no matter what country, what industry or what size company, the critical factors in every business were hiring and retaining great people. How leaders train and nurture those people define a company's culture, and these practices make each company unique.

But back in 1999, when I started the Wharton MBA program, I thought I knew it all. If you asked me to jot down the most strategic assets or competitive advantages for an organization, I would've listed things like:

Customers

Product

Strategy

Marketing

Distribution

Thirteen years later, I realized how I got it all wrong. Success starts with people and culture. If I take care of my people, they'll take care of customers, and customers will then take care of the organization. It's that simple.

Finding my Entrepreneurial Happiness

Interviewing entrepreneurs helped focus my personal introspection in a very cathartic way. I saw pieces of my own burnout in those that I spoke with, and I could empathize with their struggles. Almost all the entrepreneurs I interviewed had a few things in common with each other:

a) Their main competitive advantage was their people

b) They experienced pain around managing their people

c) Each recognized the need to maintain a positive culture

It was clear to me that happier employees lead to less-stressed business owners. Happy employees are more productive, have fewer absences, deliver better customer service, and stay with the organization longer. When you couple increased productivity with happier people, the result is typically a more profitable business.

But the striking thing I discovered is that happier employees make happier bosses!

My proof is looking no further than TINYhr. I've never been so happy, and I know my team is one of the happiest in the world based on TINYpulse benchmarks.

Meanwhile, I'm now active on the board of BuddyTV without playing a direct role within the company, and they are thriving in a new direction. I'm glad that I could be honest with myself and Andy so that they could bring in new energy.

For me, I know hiring and keeping the right people and creating a healthy and energetic culture that enables those people to thrive is my most important role as an entrepreneur. Like our values state, I jealously treasure and guard our culture because great cultures can erode over time without the right nurturing, investment, and vigilance. My vigilance is not always easy to uphold, but keeping this fantastic culture is rewarding, and it makes me happy.

Walking the Talk

I've tried many of the tips shared by the entrepreneurs from my interviews. As a result of these best practices, our TINY team excels as we focus on making employees happier.

Within months of launching TINYpulse publicly, we had hundreds of paying clients that range from Fortune 500 companies to startups to non-profits to governmental agencies. Over 1/3 of our clients are outside of the U.S. which highlights that employee happiness isn't just a Western management issue—it's a global problem and opportunity. I'm humbled by all the thank you notes we get from not only CEOs but employees on how TINYpulse is sparking positive change at their workplace. There's nothing I'd rather be doing. I'm loving it!

It reminds me that there's never a perfect time to do things that require time, risk and sacrifice—but not taking the shot only leads to regrets. If I didn't go for it, TINYpulse would just be a fantasy.

If there's something you want to do that makes you anxious or that your friends think is crazy, it's probably the right time to jump.

Sure, I was scared leading up to our flight to New Zealand. I thought of all the loose ends, letting an au pair into our lives, the unfinished projects at work, the possibility of getting sick abroad, and other risks. "Are you crazy!?" began creeping through my mind. But you know what? I didn't get all the loose ends tied up, we did let an au pair into our lives, I didn't finish all the projects, and I did get sick in spades, but I would do it all over again in a heartbeat.

Thank you for coming along on my journey. I hope you enjoyed the insights, experiences, and tips that I gathered from entrepreneurs during my careercation. Finally, feel free to reach out to me personally at **david@TINYhr.com** to share your thoughts and feedback. Thanks again, and here's to your journey to find happiness!

ACKNOWLEDGEMENTS

Without so many people with me during my journey, I wouldn't have discovered happiness in the profound way that I did. I want to start by thanking my wife Alice, who made one of my life dreams come true, even when we had just started our young family. Keira, my dear daughter, you were the most adaptable of all of us. I can't wait for our next careercation together, and for you to follow dreams with your own family in the future. Kayla, thank you for believing in us and letting us watch you mature in front of our eyes. Please come visit!

Thank you to all the entrepreneurs I interviewed. You were so gracious and warm to me. Without your time, I probably would still be lost and in search of entrepreneurial happiness.

A special thanks to Cristina Key, because without you, this "book" would still be blog posts. Your energy and dedication brought us past the finish line. Thank you to John and the entire TINYhr team. I still can't believe that I get to work with such amazing people that bring me and our customers joy on a daily basis. Thanks for helping make my professional dreams come true.

I would also like to thank my father and mother, who had the "crazy" audacity to jump from Taiwan—as a high paying petroleum engineer and nurse—to America, to become a waiter and homemaker as you invested in your family and our future. Your courage inspires me and will inspire your grandchildren.

I would also like to acknowledge some friends of TINYhr that have been so supportive: Andy Liu, Forest Key, Mike Galgon, Joe Heitzeberg, Neil Patel, Cameron Herold, Kevin Nakao, Guy Kawasaki and his APE book, Entrepreneurs' Organization, and my EO forum. Thank you so much!

Finally, cheers to the hundreds of entrepreneurs and leaders who also believe it's just plain smart and the right thing to do to make your employees happier. And to the thousands of employees who TINYpulse and actively participate in stimulating positive change at your organization, I appreciate your trust and support in us, and we'll continue to strive to improve TINYpulse for you.

Here's to happier employees!

LINKS & REFERENCES

NEW ZEALAND

The Great Catering Company

http://www.greatcatering.co.nz/

https://www.facebook.com/theGreatCateringcompany

bka Interactive

http://www.bka.co.nz

https://twitter.com/bkainteractive

http://www.pinterest.com/bkainteractive/

The Professional Bar & Restaurant School

http://www.pbrs.co.nz/

https://twitter.com/PBRSHospo

Working In

http://www.workingin.com

http://www.workingin-events.com/

Stonyridge Vineyards

http://www.stonyridge.co.nz/

https://twitter.com/StonyridgeNZ

Dynamite

http://www.dynamite.co.nz/

https://twitter.com/matwylie

AUSTRALIA

Unimail/Harteffect

http://www.harteffect.com/

https://twitter.com/Harteffect_au

https://twitter.com/acculligan

Bodybolster/CityClinic

http://bodybolster.com/

https://twitter.com/BodyBolster

http://www.cityclinic.com.au/

Wedding List Co.

http://www.weddinglistco.com.au

http://www.pinterest.com/weddinglistcomp/

https://www.facebook.com/weddinglistco

The Hallway

http://www.thehallway.com.au/

https://twitter.com/juleshall

Pureprofiles

http://www.pureprofile.com/us

https://twitter.com/pureprofile

The Nile

http://www.thenile.com.au/

https://twitter.com/jethrom

Posse

https://posse.com/

http://www.rebekahcampbell.com/

https://twitter.com/rebekahposse

Koskela

http://www.koskela.com.au/

https://twitter.com/_Koskela

https://www.facebook.com/KoskelaDesign/info

Cheeky Food Group

http://www.cheekyfoodgroup.com

https://twitter.com/CheekyLeona

https://www.facebook.com/CheekyFoodGroup

GoFundraise

http://www.gofundraise.com.au/

https://twitter.com/GoFundraise

https://www.facebook.com/GoFundraise

KOREA

Incruit

http://www.incruit.com/

Asia Evolution

http://www.asiaevolution.com/

SHANGHAI

Atomic

http://www.atomic.com.cn/

https://twitter.com/ionchina

Origin Direct Asia

http://www.origindirectasia.com/

Radiance

http://www.radiance.cn/index_en.html

The Larder

http://www.linkedin.com/pub/steve-baker

VIETNAM

Vinasource

http://www.vinasource.com/

https://www.facebook.com/VinasourceVietnam

HONG KONG

Yung Kee

http://www.yungkee.com.hk/

Pacific Andes

http://www.pacificandes.com/html/index.php

agnès b DÉLICES

http://www.agnesb-delices.com

https://www.facebook.com/agnesb.delices?ref=ts

Redwolf

www.redwolfairsoft.com/

https://www.facebook.com/redwolfairsoft

U.S.A

Frontera

http://www.teamfrontera.com/company/news/

https://twitter.com/jcwdallas

Apex Facility Resources

http://www.apexfacility.com/

https://twitter.com/ApexFacility

Chameleon Technologies

http://chameleontechinc.com/

https://twitter.com/Chameleon_Tech

Avidian Technologies

https://www.avidian.com/

Wetpaint

http://www.wetpaint.com/

https://www.facebook.com/Wetpaint

https://twitter.com/elowitz

Yoogi's Closet

http://www.yoogiscloset.com/

https://twitter.com/yoogiscloset

https://www.facebook.com/YoogisCloset

Groundspeak

http://www.groundspeak.com/

http://www.geocaching.com/

https://twitter.com/GoGeocaching

Made in the USA
Charleston, SC
21 May 2014